A PORTRAIT OF THE ARTIST AS A YOUNG MAN

NOTES

including

- *Life of the Author*
- *List of Characters*
- *Brief Synopsis*
- *Introduction to the Novel*
- *Summaries & Commentaries*
- *Chapter-by-Chapter Glossaries of*
  Latin Phrases
  Irish Terms and Political Concepts
- *Character Analysis*
- *Critical Essays*
  Joyce's Use of Imagery
  The Question of Autobiography
- *Review Questions and Essay Topics*
- *Selected Bibliography*

by
Valerie Pursel Zimbaro, M.A.
University of South Florida

NEW EDITION

WILEY

Wiley Publishing, Inc.

Editor
Gary Carey, M.A., University of Colorado

Consulting Editor
James L. Roberts, Ph.D., Department of
English, University of Nebraska

Production
Wiley Indianapolis Composition Services

CliffsNotes™ *A Portrait of the Artist as a Young Man*

Published by:
Wiley Publishing, Inc.
111 River Street
Hoboken, NJ 07030
www.wiley.com

CONTENTS

A PORTRAIT OF THE ARTIST AS A YOUNG MAN

Notes

LIFE OF THE AUTHOR

Early Childhood (1882-88) James Augustine (incorrectly registered as "Augusta") Joyce was born on February 2, 1882, in the Dublin suburb of Rathgar, Ireland. Son of a dutiful mother and a charming but improvident father, Joyce was the oldest of ten surviving children; five others died in infancy. One critic has remarked, in jest, that the large number of children in the Joyce household was surpassed only by the enormous number of debts which Joyce's father incurred. Despite the family's continuous financial instability, however, Joyce's father was aware of his son's exceptional talents, and he arranged for Joyce to attend two of Ireland's most prestigious educational institutions, thereby providing his son with a solid, impressive education.

Education (1888-98) In September of 1888, Joyce began his studies at a Jesuit boarding school for boys, Clongowes Wood College. At first, he suffered from vague maladies; he felt tormented and isolated from the other boys. After a period of adjustment, both his health and his attitude improved, and soon, in spite of an occasional need of discipline by his Jesuit teachers, Joyce began to impress the Clongowes faculty with his keen memory, musical talent, and athletic ability.

Joyce returned home for his first Christmas vacation from Clongowes and found his family in turmoil because of the death of Charles Stewart Parnell, the leader of the Irish Nationalist Party. Parnell, formerly an indomitable and respected politician, had recently suffered the decline of his career as a result of his romantic involvement with a married woman, Kitty O'Shea; this highly publicized, scandalous affair resulted in his political downfall, and a year later, fervently attempting to build up a new independent party, he died of exhaustion. He was only forty-five years old.

Parnell's downfall and his subsequent death were important in Joyce's life not only because they made him aware of the disparity between Church and State in Ireland, but also because they created within the mind of a boy who had admired Parnell's heroism a fear that Ireland would always destroy its own prophets. The effect of this revelation on nine-year-old Joyce is clearly evident in "Et Tu, Healy," a poem he wrote and distributed to friends, denouncing the man who was partly responsible for Parnell's undoing.

The fall of Parnell seemed to herald yet another decline in the Joyce family fortune, and it was not long until financial reversals and a series of domestic moves made it impossible for Joyce to return to Clongowes Wood. Nonetheless, in 1893, through his father's contacts, Joyce was able to enroll in an equally prestigious day school, Belvedere College. Joyce attended school there until he was sixteen, distinguishing himself as a school leader, thespian, and award-winning essayist, whose poems and essays were published in the school magazine.

For the most part, Joyce's school years seem idyllic, but two significant events occurred when he was fourteen which helped shape the boy's spiritual and creative future. First, Joyce was admitted to, and later became the prefect of, the school's Sodality of the Blessed Virgin Mary; and second, he had his first sexual experience – with a Dublin prostitute; this paradoxical turn of events occurred within just a few weeks of each other. (Joyce's attempts to reconcile the trinity of women, sex, and creativity are woven throughout his works.) Two years later, Joyce entered University College in Dublin.

Advanced Education (1898-1903) Although University College was known as a Jesuit institution, the emphasis on religious instruction had recently been deemphasized in order to please the emerging taste for the classics. This emphasis on humanistic studies, coupled with Joyce's mature changes in temperament, enabled him to depart from religious study almost entirely; he preferred to pursue a growing interest in the myths which Wagner used for his operas. He was also fascinated by the dramas of the Norwegian playwright Henrik Ibsen.

This latter interest was not shared by the conservative members of the faculty. In fact, Joyce received considerable criticism for an essay which he delivered before the college's Literary and Historical Society, denouncing Greek and Shakespearean drama in favor of the works of more modern playwrights, such as Ibsen. Undaunted by the attacks on his aesthetic opinions, Joyce further asserted himself by revising his presentation into an essay entitled "Ibsen's New Drama," which appeared in the *Fortnightly Review* in 1900.

Throughout the remainder of Joyce's university years, he continued to take issue with popular artistic tastes. Intolerant of the emerging Irish Theater Movement, which he believed was producing offensive provincial dramas, he wrote a scathing article, "The Day of the Rabblement," in which he encouraged people to reject the paltry works of Irish dramatists and explore the works of great beauty and truth which were being produced by new European writers.

Joyce departed from University College on December 1, 1902, and traveled to Paris, where he hoped to begin a medical career and continue his writing. He soon fell behind in his studies and fell even further behind in his finances. Luckily, some of these pressures were alleviated with the help of a recent acquaintance, Lady Augusta Gregory, and a fortuitous friendship with William Butler Yeats. Both Gregory and Yeats provided Joyce with encouragement and contacts which enabled him to write reviews for Dublin's *Daily Express*.

Originally, Joyce had hoped to stay in Paris for several years, but in April 1903, his father sent him an urgent cable concerning Joyce's mother's failing health. Joyce returned to Dublin and learned that his mother had been diagnosed as dying of cirrhosis of the liver; ironically, Joyce began spending most of his time drinking and carousing with medical students. His mother finally succumbed to cancer on August 13, 1903; she was forty-four.

The Creative Years (1903-41) During the months following Mrs. Joyce's death, the household was in continuous turmoil. Joyce, however, withdrew from family problems, and on January 7, 1904, he sat down to write a piece for *Dana*, a new intellectual journal. He composed a lengthy autobiographical, satirical piece which, at his brother Stanislaus' suggestion, he entitled "A Portrait of the Artist."

A month later, the editors at *Dana* rejected the work because of its sexual content, but Joyce seized on this opportunity to develop the manuscript into a novel entitled *Stephen Hero*; the protagonist would be a Catholic artist who was both a hero and a martyr. The novel was published posthumously in 1944, and today, *Stephen Hero* is treasured because of the rich lode of autobiographical material which Joyce used for his later fictional masterpiece, *A Portrait of the Artist as a Young Man*.

In the spring of 1904, while Joyce was writing the early drafts of *Stephen Hero*, he was also writing verses for what would eventually become the collection (or suite) of thirty-six poems entitled *Chamber Music*, a work which was not published until 1907.

It was at this point in his life that Joyce met the woman whom he would love for the rest of his life, Nora Barnacle. They first met on June 10; six days later, on June 16, Joyce knew that he was in love. Thus June 16 became a special day for him, a day which he would use for the chronology of *Ulysses*. Today, Joyce fans throughout the world still celebrate June 16 as "Bloomsday."

In October 1904, Joyce and Nora moved to Zurich, where Joyce had been promised a teaching position at the Berlitz School. Arriving there, he learned that he could not be employed because the school administrators could not find a record of his application. Frustrated, Joyce decided to move to Trieste. He remained there for the next ten years and continued his writing. A son, Giorgio, was born in 1905, and a daughter, Lucia, was born in 1907.

In September 1907, Joyce began to transform *Stephen Hero* into *A Portrait of the Artist as a Young Man*, retaining "Stephen Daedalus" for the protagonist's name. It was a name which Joyce himself had already used as a pen name, and it was also a name which linked the first Christian martyr (Stephen) and the mythic Greek maze-maker (Daedalus), a man known for his cunning and skill. In addition, because Daedalus was the father of Icarus (who attempted to fly with wings fashioned by his father), the surname provided Joyce with multiple variations on the flight theme, a motif which would pervade the novel. Later, Joyce changed the spelling of the hero's last name — ostensibly, in order to deemphasize the autobiographical nature of the book.

Joyce also began working again on *Dubliners*, a book of short stories that he hoped would be a "polished looking glass" of Dublin, a mirror in which he could lamentably reflect on the intellectual, spiritual, and cultural paralysis that he believed had infected the people of Ireland. He was unsuccessful in getting *Dubliners* published and, in a sudden fit of rage, he threw the manuscript of *A Portrait* into the into the fire. Luckily, his sister Eileen was nearby and recovered it nearly intact.

Feeling that he needed to return to Ireland, Joyce took young Giorgio with him, leaving his wife and daughter behind in Trieste. He wanted to see for himself what had happened to his country of "betrayers."

Back in Dublin, not only did Joyce come to grips with the forces which had created his deep concern for Ireland, but a personal episode occurred which shaped his future works. During a meeting with an old friend and former rival for Nora's attentions, Vincent Cosgrave, Joyce became convinced that in the early days of his courting Nora, she would, after leaving Joyce for the evening, spend the rest of the evening with Cosgrave. Joyce's feelings of betrayal caused him to write a series of accusatory letters to Nora, who didn't respond at first. Later, Joyce learned from a friend that Cosgrave had lied about the incident. This revelation caused Joyce to become penitent and, in some ways, even worshipful of Nora. These letters to Nora, written during the Joyces' separation in 1909, have proven literarily significant. We know now that they provided the psychological spur, as well as the literary material, which Joyce needed to complete the final chapters of *A Portrait* and establish the essential themes for his novel *Ulysses* and his play, *Exiles*.

In 1915, after the outbreak of World War I, Joyce moved his family to Zurich, and there he finished *A Portrait* and received welcome assistance from such literary notables as William Butler Yeats and an American exile, Ezra Pound, both of whom were instrumental in *A Portrait*'s being published in serial form in *The Egoist*. The first installment appeared in 1914 on Joyce's birthday, February 2. The publication of *A Portrait* as a single volume met with difficulties, and it was only with the help of two literary patronesses, Harriet Shaw Weaver and Edith Rockefeller McCormick, that it was finally published by B. W. Huebsch in New York in 1916, and later in England by Miss Weaver's newly formed Egoist Press, in 1917. Coincidentally, *Dubliners* was also published in 1914, by Grant Richards.

In August of 1917, Joyce began to undergo a series of eye operations, surgery which would continue throughout the next fifteen years. He sustained his creative enthusiasm, nonetheless, and the serial publication of his new work, *Ulysses*, appeared in the *Little Review* in 1918 and continued through 1920.

This enormous novel, loosely structured in episodes akin to Homer's *Odyssey*, takes place during the course of a single day in the life of Leopold Bloom, a Jewish advertising canvasser, and a now-matured Stephen Dedalus. *Ulysses* revolutionized the notion of what a novel was; never before had a writer so challenged the elasticity of the English language. Immediately, critical debate raged regarding *Ulysses'* literary merit, and eventually the New York Society for the Prevention of Vice lodged an official complaint against the *Little Review* for publishing obscene material, which it identified with references to specific episodes. The result of this suit deemed *Ulysses* virtually unpublishable until Sylvia Beach, through her Shakespeare and Company bookstore, decided to undertake the production of the novel. It appeared on February 2, 1922.

The censorship of Joyce's epic whetted public interest in the work, and, at one time, one never traveled to Paris and returned home without attempting to smuggle in a copy of *Ulysses*. Until the famed Woolsey decision of 1933, *Ulysses* could not be legally admitted into the United States. In 1923, Joyce began working on *Finnegans Wake*, the enigmatic work that would consume him throughout the final years of his life. This novel, a dream-like vision of life's cycles, seems to be specifically about the past and future of man's "universal history." Essentially, the work seems to be a written revelation of the author's inner life, related in what Joyce called the "stages" of night language — with its "conscious, then semi-conscious, then unconscious" associations. Reflecting on the novel, Joyce said that the work represented a reality that was, to him, more real than everyday life. This perception of the work, however, was neither shared by his friends nor by his literary associates. The work appeared, in part, in several magazines from 1927 through 1938 and was finally published in its complete form in 1939.

The final days of Joyce's life were filled with frustration — beginning with the angry, critical reception of *Finnegans Wake* and continuing through the beginning of World War II, an event which once again necessitated Joyce's moving his family. In addition, Joyce's eyes and his general health had begun to steadily decline, and he was continually worried about the mental instability of his daughter, Lucia; she had suffered a severe mental breakdown in 1932 and was diagnosed as an incurable schizophrenic. In spite of the hopelessness of Lucia's condition, Joyce persisted in trying to find a cure for her; he felt that in some way he was responsible – that he had failed her as a father.

Joyce's own health continued to decline, and after succumbing to stomach cramps, he agreed to surgery for a previously undiagnosed duodenal ulcer; he never recovered and died on January 13, 1941. He was buried in the Fluntern Cemetery on a hill in Zurich, and his grave was decorated with only a green wreath woven in the shape of a lyre, a symbol and emblem of Ireland.

LIST OF CHARACTERS

A Portrait of the Artist as a Young Man, strictly speaking, is not an autobiographical novel, and yet in the novel, Joyce attempts to weave much of the fabric of his real life into an artful tapestry of fiction. Most of the following characters in the novel are based on people who actually existed in Joyce's life; in almost every case, he portrayed them as fictional representations of religious, social, and cultural elements of Ireland as they influenced Stephen Dedalus, a maturing, sensitive young artist.

MAIN CHARACTERS

THE DEDALUS FAMILY

Stephen Dedalus

Afflicted with poor eyesight and lacking both physical stamina and athletic prowess, Stephen develops an early, introspective, intellectual curiosity. Like many sensitive young men, Stephen is ashamed of his family's ever-strained finances. Later, he is troubled when he realizes the ineffectiveness and emptiness of both Irish nationalism and Catholicism. Eventually, Stephen feels himself becoming increasingly isolated from others. Finally, he vows to escape all forms of emotional, intellectual, and spiritual repression. He leaves Ireland for the Continent, in search of his artistic soul.

Simon Dedalus

Stephen's ineffectual father; a good-natured, but weak and

undependable man who prefers to live in the self-deluded reveries of his past rather than fulfill the role of a responsible parent. An overly sentimental, staunch Irish Nationalist, he is a poor role model for his son. Seemingly, Simon's only bit of advice for Stephen is to choose his friends well and never "peach" on them. In Chapter V, Stephen describes Simon as less a father than "a medical student, an oarsman, a tenor, an amateur actor . . . a drinker, a good fellow, a storyteller . . . and . . . a praiser of his own past."

Mary Dedalus

Stephen's mother; deeply religious and apolitical, she feels martyred by frequent pregnancy, poverty, and her burdensome, weak-willed husband. She fears that Stephen will be unhappy living abroad—away from family, friends, and the Catholic faith. She is heartbroken when he leaves Ireland at the end of the novel.

Maurice Dedalus

Stephen's younger brother. Stephen's father calls Maurice a "thickheaded ruffian." Like Stephen, Maurice is sent to Belvedere College, a Jesuit day school.

Uncle Charles

Stephen's granduncle (great-uncle) who lives with the Dedalus family. He is an aging, "hale old man with welltanned skin, rugged features and white side whiskers." He spends memorable mornings walking with young Stephen, visiting neighboring vendors and pilfering items for Stephen's consumption. A relic of Ireland's hearty and spirited past, Uncle Charles resides with the family until his death.

Aunt Dante (Mrs. Riordan)

Not an aunt by blood or by marriage, this "well-read, clever," and overzealous Irish governess of the Dedalus children values "God and religion before everything!" During Stephen's first Christmas dinner with the adults in his household, Dante's firm religious convictions clash violently with Mr. Casey's political opinions regarding Charles Stewart Parnell. Her final denunciation of Parnell, directed at Simon and Mr. Casey, leaves both men weeping over the fate of their fallen leader and the precarious future of their country.

Katey, Maggy, and Boody Dedalus

Stephen's younger sisters. They appear only momentarily in Chapter V as they help Stephen get ready to leave for the university.

OTHER CHARACTERS

Mr. (John) Casey

A close friend of Simon Dedalus, he is present at a climactic Christmas dinner, where he engages in a heated argument with Mrs. Riordan about Charles Stewart Parnell. A devoted supporter of the Nationalist cause, and one who has been jailed on several occasions for making public speeches in favor of Parnell, Casey expresses his resentment against the local clergy who used the pulpit and confessionals to whip Parnell with the scourge of immorality, thereby subverting his political effectiveness. Parnell's highly publicized affair with Kitty O'Shea led to the downfall of his once-glorious political career.

Eileen Vance

The daughter of the Dedaluses' Protestant neighbors. As a young child, Stephen said that he was going to marry Eileen; Dante was livid, and instantly and firmly, she discouraged the possibility of such a "sinful" association. Thus, a pattern was begun. For young Stephen, Eileen was the first in a long line of women who were desired by Stephen but who were condemned by other people for one reason or another. Specifically, Stephen remembers Eileen's cool, soft, "long white hands"; the image of Eileen's hands enables Stephen to understand the meaning of the term "Tower of Ivory," a phrase which he had often repeated without comprehension in the Litany to the Blessed Virgin Mary. Eileen's characteristics eventually blend with other female "E" references in the novel—"Emma" and "E–C–" and Emma Clery—all revealing different facets of Stephen's ambiguous, confused, conflicting sentiments about the women in his life.

CLONGOWES WOOD COLLEGE (Chapter I)

Father Arnall

A stern, intolerant, easily angered Latin teacher who punishes Stephen's friend Fleming for writing a poor Latin theme by making him kneel in the middle of the classroom floor. He appears later in Chapter III as the retreat master who delivers the "fire and brimstone" Judgment Day sermons.

Father Dolan

The bespectacled, arrogant and sadistic prefect of studies whom Stephen describes with a variety of rat-like characteristics, including a "whitegrey face and [cruel] noncolored eyes." Dolan humiliates Stephen by accusing him of avoiding Latin classwork, even though Stephen explains that he broke his glasses. The prefect calls Stephen's answer an "old schoolboy trick" and punishes him by violently smacking his palms with a pandybat. Afterward, Stephen begins to doubt the integrity of those in the clerical professions.

Father Conmee

The charitable rector of the school; he has a "kindlooking face" and "a cool, moist palm." Stephen seeks his counsel regarding the unfair pandying incident. Father Conmee is just and compassionate, and he assuages Stephen's doubts by excusing him from work pending the arrival of his new glasses. He also promises to resolve the unfortunate matter with Father Dolan. Later, however, Father Conmee's duplicity is revealed; we learn that he regarded the pandying incident as a joke, laughing broadly about it with Stephen's father. Stephen learns about the laughter and, once again, he feels betrayed by his father, by the Jesuits, and, by extension, by the Church.

Brother Michael

A cheerful, "reddish grey hair[ed]" attendant who cares for Stephen during his stint in the school infirmary. Brother Michael is a nonthreatening authority figure for whom Stephen feels pity because of Brother Michael's sadness as he reads aloud the newspaper article about Parnell's death.

Fleming

A "decent," attentive, and reassuring friend to Stephen. He is the first to notice Stephen's ensuing illness after the ditch incident, and it is he who writes a playful verse on one of Stephen's textbooks, confirming Stephen's presence in the universe. Later, like Stephen, Fleming is pandied for what his teacher perceives as idleness.

Jack Lawton

A friendly rival of Stephen's; he is head of the Lancaster scholastic team, which is pitted against Stephen's Yorkist team.

Nasty Roche

The wealthy, pampered son of a magistrate; he is the first person to question Stephen about his family and about his unusual name. Later, Roche is so angered by Father Dolan's unfair attack on Stephen that he encourages Stephen to visit the rector, Father Conmee, and defend himself.

Wells

An abrasive, unruly student who mocks Stephen's sensitivity with questions about whether or not Stephen kisses his mother. Later, he pushes Stephen into the "square ditch" (a cesspool); as a result, Stephen develops a fever and has to be admitted to the school infirmary.

Athy

The son of a racehorse owner; he befriends Stephen during his stay in the infirmary. He shares Stephen's affection for Brother Michael and admits that he, like Stephen, also has an unusual last name.

Rody Kickham, Cecil Thunder, Simon Moonan, Hamilton Rowan, Dominic Kelly, Tusker Boyle, Jimmy Magee, Paddy Rath, Corrigan, Cantwell, Saurin and Anthony McSwiney

Other students at Clongowes Wood College; they serve as foils and sharp contrasts to Stephen. They represent the opposite of Stephen's artistic temperament and introspective behavior. For the most part, they are either crude, disrespectful, or overtly physical.

Aubrey Mills

He becomes Stephen's friend and summer companion. Together, they pursue many adventures – exploring gardens, dueling on the seaside rocks, and taking turns riding a mare amidst the cows on a dairy farm. Their exploits provide a carefree, bucolic memory of Stephen's summer at Blackrock before he enters Belvedere College.

Mike Flynn

A decrepit friend of Simon Dedalus; he has tobacco-stained fingers, a "flabby stubblecovered face [and] lusterless blue eyes"; he acts as Stephen's "track trainer" during Stephen's summer at Blackrock.

BELVEDERE COLLEGE (Chapters II–IV)

Vincent Heron

With a "high, throaty voice" and a "pale dandyish face," Vincent has the name and appearance of a bird. He is Stephen's friendly rival as a leader at Belvedere; he often ridicules Stephen for his overly conservative attitudes and behavior.

Wallis

A close friend and loyal follower of Vincent Heron. Although he tries to imitate Heron's mannerisms and cavalier attitude, he is uncomfortable and generally unsuccessful in his efforts.

Bertie Tallon

He is a subject of ridicule during the school play because he has to take the role of a sunbonneted girl, which necessitates his wearing a wig, makeup, and performing a solo dance.

Boland

A boy with a "large grin"; Stephen refers to him as "a dunce." He is a typical bully and taunts Stephen into discussing his favorite poet.

Nash

Stephen's classmate with a "great red head"; he is a close friend of Boland. Stephen calls Nash an "idler." Nash's assertion that Tennyson is a better poet than Byron causes Stephen to respond vehemently.

Father Arnall

The Jesuit priest who pandied Fleming in Latin class (Chapter I). In Chapter II, he conducts a three-day religious retreat. His vivid hellfire-and-brimstone "spiritual exercises" scare the wits out of Stephen and cause him to seek immediate absolution for his sins.

Johnny Cashman

A "brisk old man"; an old friend of Simon Dedalus. Stephen finds the old man's humor offensive; he is particularly disgusted by his portrayal of Simon and Stephen's great-grandfather as womanizers and heavy drinkers.

UNIVERSITY COLLEGE, DUBLIN (Chapter V)

Dean of Studies

An English Jesuit priest who has a discussion with Stephen regarding the difference between moral beauty and material beauty. While discussing Stephen's preference for Aristotle and Aquinas, the dean says that he himself prefers a more "practical" application of the arts to Stephen's "liberal" interest in them. Compared to Stephen, the dean's views are pedestrian and lack philosophical insight.

Cranly

Stephen's humanitarian friend with the "priestlike face" and "womanish eyes"; Stephen confides the "tumults and unrests and longings in his soul" to Cranly. Cranly fears the sense of loneliness that Stephen seems to welcome (and even accept) as an essential part of an artist's life, and he warns Stephen about the dangers of alienation and faithlessness, urging him to reconsider his decision to leave Ireland.

Lynch

Stephen's irreverent, crude, and superficial friend, whose reptilian eyes reveal a "shriveling" soul. During one of their walks together, Stephen uses Lynch as a sounding board, explaining his theory about two philosophical definitions not addressed by Aristotle. As he talks with Lynch, he explains his personal theory of aesthetics.

Davin

A solid, provincial Irish peasant lad; Stephen's friend and fellow student. Davin's fierce Irish nationalism reveals both the intensity and violence in the lives of the Irish peasant class and is proof, to Stephen, that a life of unquestioned patriotism is one to be avoided.

MacCann

A "squat figure" and "self-proclaimed democrat" dedicated to circulating a petition in favor of "social liberty and equality among all classes and sexes in the United States of Europe of the future." Because Stephen refuses to conform to MacCann's demonstrative social conscience, MacCann labels Stephen an egocentric elitist.

Temple

A highly emotional "gypsy student" who admires Stephen's keen intellect and passionate individuality. Temple respects Stephen's decision not to sign MacCann's petition, and he uses this issue to emphasize his open dislike of Cranly.

Moynihan, MacAlister, Donovan, Dixon, O'Keefe, Goggins, Glynn, Shuley, Ennis, and Connelly

These young men represent the intellectual and cultural diversity of Dublin's typical University College students, from whom Stephen differentiates himself both in attitudes and in actions.

BRIEF SYNOPSIS

The novel begins with Stephen Dedalus' first memories, when he was about three years old. The fragmented lines are from a childhood story and a nursery song and are linked with family associations, sensory perceptions, and pieces of conversation. In this opening scene, Joyce is presenting to us the genesis of a future artist's perception and interpretation of the world.

Moving from Stephen's infancy to his early days at Clongowes Wood College, a Jesuit boarding school for boys, Joyce focuses on three key incidents which significantly affect Stephen's personality. First, Stephen is pushed into an open cesspool by a bullying classmate, and, subsequently, he develops a fever which confines him to the school infirmary; here, he begins to discern that he is "different," that he is an outsider.

Later, when he is probably six years old, Stephen returns home to celebrate Christmas dinner with his family and is invited, for the first time, to sit with the adults at the dinner table. This extraordinarily happy occasion is marred by a heated political argument between Stephen's old nurse, Dante Riordan, and a dinner guest, Mr. Casey, leaving Stephen confused about the issues of religion and politics in the adult world.

On returning to school, Stephen accidentally breaks his glasses and is unable to complete his classwork. He is unjustly humiliated and punished by the cruel prefect of studies, but after receiving encouragement from a friend, Stephen bravely (if fearfully) goes to the rector of the school and obtains justice. The success of this meeting instills in him a healthy self-confidence and ennobles him, for a moment, in the eyes of his classmates.

After a brief summer vacation at his home in Blackrock, Stephen learns that his father's financial reversals make it impossible to return to Clongowes Wood; instead, he is enrolled in a less prestigious Jesuit day school, Belvedere College. Here, he develops a distinguished reputation as an award-winning essay writer and a fine actor in his school play. Despite these accomplishments, however, Stephen feels increasingly alienated from his schoolmates because of his growing religious skepticism and his deep interest in literature and writing. This feeling of isolation is intensified during a trip with his father to Cork, where he learns more about his father's weaknesses.

Stephen becomes increasingly repelled by the dead-end realities of Dublin life. Frustrated by his loss of faith in the Catholic Church, in his family situation, and in his cultural bonds, Stephen seeks to "appease the fierce longings of his heart." After wandering through the city's brothel district, he finds momentary solace with a Dublin prostitute. He is fourteen years old, and this is his first sexual experience.

After a period of "sinful living," Stephen attends an intense three-day spiritual retreat. During that time, he is overwhelmed by guilt and remorse; he believes that Father Arnall is speaking directly to him. Panicking, he seeks out a kindly old Capuchin priest, pledges moral reform, and rededicates himself to a life of purity and devotion. He fills his days with fervent prayers and takes part in as many religious services as he can.

Noticing Stephen's exceedingly pious behavior, the director of the school arranges a meeting to encourage Stephen to consider entering the priesthood. At first, Stephen is flattered, fascinated by the possibilities of the clerical life, but increasingly he is tormented by carnal desires. He finally realizes that his "inherent sinful nature" makes it necessary for him to reject a religious vocation.

Having made this discovery about himself, Stephen decides to enroll in the university, where he hopes to shape his destiny as an artist. This decision is immediately followed by a climactic "epiphany": he sees a girl wading in the sea; to Stephen, she embodies the attraction, the promise, and the abandon which he wishes to experience in life. It is at this moment that Stephen understands that he can only hope to gain this experience through a life of artistic expression.

Shortly thereafter, Stephen begins a new life as a young man in search of his own values and his own credo. In comparison with the other college students, Stephen often seems anti-social and more concerned with pursuing his own interests than supporting the causes of others. Even Stephen himself realizes that unlike most of his friends, he is unusually introspective. He is not the typical devil-may-care university student; he rejects the typical blind patriotic blather, and although he continues to respect the Catholic faith, he no longer believes that its tenets should govern his life. Through conversations with friends and a dean of studies, Stephen eventually develops his own aesthetic theory of art, based on the philosophies of Aristotle and Aquinas. Simultaneously, he concludes that if he is ever going to find his artistic soul, he must sever all bonds of faith, family, and country. He must leave Dublin and go abroad to "forge" his soul's "uncreated conscience."

INTRODUCTION TO THE NOVEL

A Portrait of the Artist as a Young Man details events which closely correspond with those of Joyce's first twenty years. According to Joyce's celebrated biographer, Richard Ellman, Joyce hoped that his *Portrait* would be an **autobiographical novel**, "turning his life into fiction." While scholars disagree on the extent to which Joyce's life affected his fictional narrative in the novel, most of them concur that Stephen Dedalus is both the **protagonist** of the novel, as well as the **persona** (Latin, meaning "mask") behind which Joyce paints his fictional "portrait" of the "artist" and of the "young man."

A close examination of these obvious clues in the title reveals to readers that the novel can be classified as both a **Kunstlerroman** (German, meaning a novel about an artist) and a **Bildungsroman** (German, meaning a novel of development or education). If we understand these terms, we can more clearly understand Joyce's primary purpose for writing the novel.

We must keep in mind, however, that many of the people and the situations of the novel have been presented in the form of **satire**. We must also be aware that the author selected this technique to emphasize how the life of an artist differs from that of others who share his world.

In *A Portrait*, the reader learns through the particular experiences of Stephen Dedalus how an artist perceives his surroundings, as well as his views on faith, family, and country, and how these perceptions often conflict with those prescribed for him by society. As a result, the artist feels distanced from the world. Unfortunately, this feeling of distance and detachment is misconstrued by others to be the prideful attitude of an egoist. Thus the artist, already feeling isolated, is increasingly aware of a certain growing, painful social **alienation**.

In addition, Stephen's natural, maturing sexual urges confuse him even further. Stephen is a keenly intelligent, sensitive, and eloquent young man, but he also possesses the feelings of urgent sexuality, self-doubt, and insecurity—all universal emotions which are experienced during the development of the average adolescent male. Joyce reveals these tumultuous adolescent feelings through a narrative technique called **stream-of-consciousness**. He takes the reader into both the conscious mind and the subconscious mind, showing him the subjective and the objective realities of a situation. Using Stephen Dedalus, he explores the depths of the human heart.

This novel is narrated, for the most part, in the **limited omniscient point of view**; at the same time, it progresses in form from the lyrical and epical modes of expression and moves finally into the dramatic mode of expression. (These "modes of expression" are Stephen's own terms, defining the various kinds of literature; when we encounter them in the novel, we should write down Stephen's definitions and attempt to chart the course of this novel according to its evolving lyrical, epical, and dramatic levels.)

Stephen's thoughts, associations, feelings, and language (both cerebral and verbal) serve as the primary vehicles by which the reader shares with Stephen the pain and pleasures of adolescence, as well as the exhilarating experiences of intellectual, sexual, and spiritual discoveries.

In order to highlight the importance of Stephen's aesthetic experiences, Joyce borrowed a word from the Catholic faith in order to create a literary term of his own. When Stephen suddenly understands "the essential nature of a thing"–whether it is the understanding of a person, an idea, a word, or a situation – he has a moment of profound revelation. Joyce called these moments **epiphanies**.

Some of Stephen's earliest epiphanies come from his acute sensory awareness and are recorded through Joyce's masterful use of imagery. In the novel, repeated patterns of sounds and remembrances of tastes, touches, and smells are all emphasized. Stephen's eyesight (like Joyce's) is weak; therefore, Joyce emphasizes other senses, and in doing so, he employs the valuable **motif** method of narration, wherein he records recurrent images of hot/cold, wet/dry, and light/dark images, as well as recurring symbols. He also uses **dramatic irony** to identify Stephen's basic conflicts and emphasize significant events in his life.

Although several themes such as alienation and betrayal exist in the novel, Ellman states that Joyce originally recognized the work's main **theme** as "the portrait of the renegade Catholic artist as hero." Certainly, evidence from Joyce's life mirrors Stephen's need to escape the bonds of Irish nationalism and Catholicism, both of which seemed to threaten his pursuit of a literary career.

The most obvious clue that the author's life is related to the novel's thematic development exists in the hero's name – Stephen Dedalus, which combines significant elements of both Greek and Christian **myths**. "Stephen" is the name of the first Christian martyr who was persecuted for reasons of faith. Joyce's hero identifies with his patron's martyrdom by recalling an early reprimand against marrying a Protestant, the unjust pandying incident, and a variety of instances wherein he was ostracized or made to feel guilty by his peers and older people.

It is, however, the author's choice of his character's family name — Dedalus — which reveals to readers the source of the novel's greatest thematic parallel. The myth of Daedalus and Icarus, the story of the cunning Greek inventor and his ill-fated, impetuous son, is the framework responsible for the major imagery and symbolism which pervade the novel.

Daedalus, an architect commissioned by King Minos, designed an elaborate labyrinth in which the king planned to confine the monstrous Minotaur. However, ill-fortune soon caused Daedalus and Icarus to be imprisoned in the labyrinth, from which they were forced to contrive a daring and ingenious escape.

Symbolically, Stephen, like Daedalus, feels compelled to find a means of escape from the labyrinth of Dublin which threatens him with spiritual, cultural, and artistic restraints. Similarly, Stephen can also be compared with Icarus, who flew too close to the sun, melted his fabricated wings, and plunged to his death in the sea. Like Icarus, Stephen ignores the warnings of family and clergy and is symbolically drawn toward a philosophical illumination which ultimately casts him into sin (spiritual death) and leads him to renounce his Catholic faith.

The final and most dramatic parallel associates Stephen with his mythic namesake Daedalus — the "great artificer." Like Daedalus, Stephen succeeds in escaping the labyrinth of cultural restraints. At the end of the novel, Stephen is imaginatively soaring — in flight away from Ireland toward a future of unfettered artistic freedom.

SUMMARIES AND COMMENTARIES

CHAPTER I

Summary

When the novel opens, we are in the mind of a child; fragmented lines from a nursery story are intertwined with sensations and associations of feeling, touching, hearing, and smelling. Joyce takes us inside the mind of a child in order to show us how a child records and responds to the world around him. By carefully choosing language and syntax, Joyce enables us to share what is possibly the earliest childhood memory of the novel's hero – Stephen Dedalus.

Stephen is only three years old when he begins to identify himself with the physical world, with members of his family, and with the sensual world of language; he remembers his father's hairy face, his mother's sweet smell, the uncomfortable experience of wetting the bed, and certain special and fanciful words, such as "baby tuckoo" and "moocow." It was a good time, he says, meaning that he felt safe and secure from harm. Significantly, his favorite song is about *wild* roses – not tamed, cultivated roses, but wild roses. His taste for rebellion and freedom has already budded.

Stephen's next memory occurs about three years later, when he attempts to compete athletically with a group of rowdy schoolmates at Clongowes Wood College, the Jesuit boarding school which he attends. By comparison with the other boys, Stephen is small and weak and suffers from poor vision and painful homesickness. During these miserable days, he comforts himself with thoughts of home. As he thinks about these things, it is clear that Stephen is a lonely, sensitive young boy, one who loves learning and relies on the strength he receives from saying his evening prayers.

Stephen's first crisis at Clongowes occurs when Wells, a bullying classmate, pushes Stephen into the square ditch (a cesspool), causing him to be taken to the school infirmary to recover from a fever. While there, Stephen meets Athy, the likeable son of a racehorse owner; Athy confides to Stephen that he too has an unusual name. While Stephen is in the Infirmary, he also meets the somewhat sad but compassionate cleric Brother Michael, who cares for sick boys and makes them feel less isolated by reading them the news in the daily paper.

Although Stephen feels depressed by his illness, he comforts himself by melodramatically imagining the beauty of his own burial ceremony and Wells' great remorse for having caused Stephen's unfortunate death. Then Stephen falls into a fitful sleep; he is lulled by "waves" of light, the sounds of imaginary sea waves, and the words which Brother Michael is reading about the death of Charles Stewart Parnell, the young, romantic Irish hero.

Parnell's death becomes more significant in the following scene, when Stephen returns home to celebrate Christmas. At the Christmas dinner are Stephen's parents (Mary and Simon), John Casey (a friend of Simon's), Stephen's greatuncle Charles, and Stephen's old nurse, Dante Riordan. Stephen is particularly excited because for the first time in his life, he is sitting at the table with the adults.

The joy of the occasion is soon interrupted, however, by an argument about the Catholic Church's role in politics and its attitude toward the followers of the late Irish Nationalist, Charles Stewart Parnell.

Casey, a staunch supporter of Parnell's cause, defends Parnell against the injustices committed against him and his cause by the Irish people and by the Catholic Church. According to Casey, the Church hounded Parnell into his grave. The argument naturally includes mention of Parnell's highly publicized love affair with a married woman, Kitty O'Shea, and Dante Riordan vehemently defends the Church's censure of Parnell's involvement with Kitty. Casey says that because the Church interfered with secular matters, it thereby ended a political career which had seemed to promise Home Rule for Ireland.

The argument escalates with an exchange of insults and concludes with Dante's triumphantly shouting, "We crushed him [Parnell] to death!" She slams the door, leaving Simon and Casey weeping over the loss of their beloved hero.

The next scene opens with Stephen back at Clongowes, overhearing a conversation about the punishment awaiting some students who stole some altar wine from the sacristy. Thinking about the dark, silent sacristy and sacred things in general, Stephen suddenly envisions Eileen Vance, a young girl with hands like ivory, so smooth that they remind him of two worshipful phrases that he repeats during the Litany to the Blessed Virgin—"Tower of Ivory" and "House of Gold." Suddenly, Stephen's musings are interrupted by a call to class.

During Father Arnall's Latin lesson, Father Dolan, the prefect of studies, who wields the menacing pandybat in search of "lazy idle little loafers," appears. Dolan notices that Fleming and Stephen are not doing their lessons. After disciplining Fleming, Dolan approaches Stephen, who explains that he has been excused temporarily from his assignments because he broke his glasses.

Refusing to believe that Stephen broke them accidentally, the cynical, sadistic Dolan commands the boy to put out his hands for "pandying." This punishment, according to Dolan, is demanded for idleness and schoolboy tricks. Afterward, Stephen feels humiliated and angered by the unjust cruelty. His classmates are angered too; they believe that Stephen should report the prefect's injustice to the rector of the school.

Stephen briefly considers the consequences of such a bold action; then he sets out, following the winding corridors that lead to "the castle." He confronts the rector with the truth about the broken glasses, and, to Stephen's amazement, the rector, Father Conmee, is both sympathetic and kind; he promises to resolve the situation with Father Dolan on Stephen's behalf. Comforted and exhilarated by the results of the meeting, Stephen rushes from the gloomy corridors of the castle to be greeted by his classmates as a leader and a hero. They lock hands and lift him heavenward. Metaphorically, Stephen is flying, momentarily free of fear and constraint.

Commentary

At the beginning of the novel, we meet Stephen at the moment when he experiences his first essential awareness of the world around him. He is "baby tuckoo," the center of the universe, the one to whom stories are told and songs are sung. We perceive the world exactly as Stephen does – through sounds, smells, and sensations – all structured by a catalogue of comparisons which introduce the novel's good/bad, cold/hot, light/dark image motifs.

Clearly, even at an early age, Stephen prefers his mother to his father, and he is unconsciously aware of his nurse Dante's political and religious ideologies. He also learns, because of the "Pull out his eyes, Apologise . . . " refrain, that any sudden, natural (spontaneous, artistic) expression of emotion – such as his declaration that he is going to marry Eileen (a little Protestant girl) – will result in swift moral retribution from the stern and practical members of his family. Later, of course, society's censures will parallel Stephen's family's early condemnation of his spontaneous outbursts of emotion and artistic expression.

Stephen's overly sensitive reactions to this censoring incident is proof to us that Stephen is "different." He feels keenly guilty without understanding why; later in life, he will suffer other moments of agonizing, confusing guilt.

The next scene, at Clongowes, focuses on Stephen's growing sense of isolation. Joyce's imagery in this passage –"swarming . . . strong cries . . . pale and chilly . . . thud . . . [and] greasy . . ."– indicates

Stephen's general discomfort in his new surroundings. The use of the term "heavy bird," describing the low-flying, ponderous football, introduces bird imagery, imagery which will pervade the novel; here, it is used to identify the mythical escape theme which unifies the novel. Young Dedalus (like his Greek namesake, Daedalus) sees himself in a hostile environment from which, at least for the moment, he is unlikely to escape, although he would like to. Similarly, Stephen (the name of the first Christian martyr) suffers ridicule because of the uniqueness of his name; he is mercilessly questioned about his name by a bullying classmate, Nasty Roche.

Stephen's feelings of loneliness increase as he thinks of the day when his parents said good-bye to him, leaving him helpless in the threatening maze of his new life at Clongowes, where he felt "caught in the whirl of a scrimmage . . . fearful of the flashing eyes and muddy boots . . . " He soon realizes that he can momentarily escape the cruel realities of school life by contemplating things which he finds beautiful and, later, re-creating them with words.

For example, when reflecting on the lighted castle, Stephen remarks, "It was like something in a book." Here, Stephen reveals an early insight into the nature of creativity: he can translate something physical into artistic form. He not only begins to value words, but he also realizes that a particular arrangement of words makes the "nice sentences in Doctor Cornwell's Spelling Book" seem "like poetry." Stephen is already a young artist. This scene plays an important part in Joyce's revelation of Stephen's ultimate escape from a humdrum, priest-ridden life.

Suddenly, Stephen's artistic reverie is interrupted by real life, and we are reminded that although Stephen may be artistic, he is still a little boy. Stephen precisely describes the disgusting details of being pushed into the "square ditch" by a bullying classmate, and, here, in addition to our responding to Stephen's description of the sensations he felt, we should be aware that the sudden shock of the cold, slimy [cesspool] water is heavily symbolic; the submersion into the cesspool is Stephen's crude baptism into an offensive and cruel world, a world which differs greatly from the warm, secure world of home. The contrast between these two worlds, as well as the contrast between a series of hot/cold images (hot is natural and therefore good; cold is unfeeling and therefore bad), sets up another catalogue of comparisons and conflicts which Stephen must try to resolve as he attempts to find his place in the new world of Clongowes.

One of the conflicts which Stephen must face is the class competition between the scholastic teams of York and Lancaster, named after the British royal families involved in the War of the Roses (1445-85). Although the team badges, bearing either a red or white rose, represent two political factions, Stephen is not really concerned with winning the scholastic contest. He is concentrating on a world which might allow the limitless possibilities of "wild rose blossoms." Here, as he will do in future years, Stephen shuns the arbitrary restrictions governing religion and/or politics; he prefers, instead, to re-create (in his mind) a more tolerant world in which he can feel free to express his own wild, creative nature.

In addition to introducing us to Stephen's "differentness" and his feelings of alienation, Joyce is also introducing us to the matter of loyalty—in particular, the matter of Stephen's loyalty to his "mother country," Ireland. The character who most represents Ireland is Stephen's mother, Mary Dedalus, and Stephen's later anxieties about exile from Mother Ireland are foreshadowed here in his thoughts about being exiled from his loving mother while he is at boarding school. Feeling alien and alone, Stephen longs to be "at home [where he can] lay his head on his mother's lap." This longing troubles Stephen, and one night as he waits for sleep, he begins to imaginatively open and close the flaps of his ears, creating a Freudian-like sensation of a "train going into a tunnel." Freud's imagery, not unfamiliar to Joyce, is related not only to the experience of childbirth, but it also is related to the anxiety/release pattern which Stephen is experiencing because of his separation from home. These anxieties increase when Wells asks Stephen about kissing his mother. Once again, unable to understand his feelings of hot guilt, Stephen finds solace in the beauty and precision of words.

One day, while contemplating his loneliness, Stephen begins to graphically establish his own sense of identity by writing in his lesson book, "Stephen Dedalus/ Class of Elements/ Clongowes Wood College/ Sallins/ County Kildare/ Ireland/ Europe/ The World/ The Universe." This declaration of identity, illustrating his feelings of smallness in an immense world, marks the beginning of Stephen's attempt to consciously arrange the details of his life in his own manner, to creatively establish control, using the power of words in a pattern.

There exists, however, an area of conflict that Stephen cannot resolve by resorting to words. Religion is a problem for the young boy. He finds comfort in the repetition of memorized prayers; he is offered solace, but, at the same time, he is terrified by the notion of the eternal fires of eternal damnation. In the scene when Stephen recites his prayers before going to bed, Joyce conveys his own disdain for the rote memorizations encouraged by the Catholic Church. Such prayers, he believes, offer small hope for people who are deeply troubled; ultimately, such prayers are of little use in times of deep suffering. Stephen's own prayers seem to echo Joyce's observations; it is likely that the boy does not even understand the prayers that he is reciting. Note that his night tremblings seem to cease not *after* prayers, but *after* he reminds himself that he will not go to hell when he dies. However, Stephen is not *truly* comforted. He is still haunted by the terrible image of the prefect's descent down a dark, mythical corridor. Stephen's night fears dissolve only *after* he remembers that he will soon be going home for the holidays.

Feeling feverish after falling in the square ditch, Stephen realizes that a hand is on his forehead, and he begins to hallucinate that the cold, clammy hand and the beady little eyes that he sees are those of a rat. This preoccupation with rodents leads him to think about dead rats, dead things in general, and ultimately about his own death. In a vivid stream-of-consciousness passage, Stephen begins to contemplate the beauty of his own burial ceremony, fantasizing how greatly he will be missed.

Stephen's thoughts return to reality with the sudden appearance of Brother Michael, a kindly cleric charged with taking care of boys in the infirmary. The fact that Brother Michael is not a priest, like the other clerics in the school, makes Stephen wonder whether Brother Michael's kindness differentiates him from the others; Stephen wonders if Brother Michael is less holy because of his kindness.

While Stephen is in the infirmary, he meets Athy, the affable son of a racehorse owner; unlike Stephen, Athy seems to enjoy the uniqueness of having a "queer name." The infirmary can thus be considered a microcosm for those like Stephen. That is, Brother Michael, Athy, and Stephen are all isolated – either by duties, names, or physical illness from the rest of the world of Clongowes.

Stephen contemplates his feelings of isolation as he falls asleep, lulled by pleasant memories of home and the sad sound of Brother

Michael's voice as it reveals the news from the daily paper that Charles Stewart Parnell, the Irish Nationalist leader, is dead. In his dream, Stephen's preoccupation with his illness and his fears of death merge with his thoughts about Parnell's death, and he begins to identify his own plight with that of the great, rejected Irish hero.

When the next scene opens, Stephen is well and happy; he is back home in Bray with his family, just as they are about to sit down for Christmas dinner. It is a momentous occasion; this meal will be Stephen's ceremonial initiation into the adult world. By being allowed to say grace before the meal, Stephen has joined the world of grown-ups, a world which he expects will be filled with the excitement, joy, and peace of the season. Ironically, this dinner which is traditionally held to announce the joyous anniversary of the birth of the Savior of the World becomes the scene of loud, vindictive, religious and political debate. Ultimately, its angry focus is not on a birth, but on the death of a man who seemingly was once Ireland's savior, Ireland's hope for independence from England, Ireland's best hope for Home Rule.

In a sense, this traumatic experience causes Stephen to confront some of the disappointing truths about the adult members of his household. Dante, his old nurse and governess, a woman whom he has loved as if she were an aunt, is rigid and cruel as she loudly defends her faith and the Church's interference with matters of the state. Interestingly, this scene is based on an actual occurrence in the Joyce household. Dante Conway (the Joyce children's governess) and a Mr. John Kelley (a friend of Joyce's father who had been imprisoned for giving public speeches in defense of Parnell) actually did have a loud, angry argument during a Christmas dinner when Joyce was a boy. The vicious screaming ingrained itself so deeply in Joyce's memory that he was able to re-create its strong, minute details here. As a result of the argument, Stephen realizes that the pursuit of freedom usually includes martyrdom—a situation enunciated by Joyce himself, a belief that Ireland would always destroy her heroes.

This emotionally traumatic Christmas dinner, the climax of Chapter I, marks the beginning of Stephen's loss of innocence. Increasingly, Stephen will begin to view the world with more cynicism and apathy, and before long, he will begin to expect disillusionment in areas of life which he once held sacred. Such is the case when he returns to school and the other children seem to be "smaller and farther away" than they did before. He listens to the fears of his classmates as they discuss the fate of the boys accused of stealing wine from the sacristy, but the details of the sacrilege no longer seem to shock him. Instead, Stephen tries to make sense of his new perspective by relying on the familiar rhythms of the Litany of the Blessed Virgin. For the first time, he begins to examine the actual meaning of the words which he has routinely, unthinkingly, repeated for years. He begins to understand the words not so much for their piety, but for their beauty as art.

In contrast to Stephen's discovering the beauty of the words in the Litany, Joyce juxtaposes the unfair, cruel reality of the Catholic Church, represented by Father Dolan. In careful detail, Joyce re-creates the sound and the motion of Father Dolan's pandybat, as well as the feelings associated with being smacked with the pandybat. Joyce is foreshadowing here what will eventually happen to Stephen, and, as a result, we will more deeply share Stephen's painful, unjust punishment.

Initially, of course, Stephen never suspects the potential cruelty of Father Dolan. Stephen has suffered from the cruelty of his classmates — specifically, he was pushed in the filthy ditch of water and, later, a classmate caused him to break his glasses on the cinderpath — but Stephen has yet to experience injustice from a cleric, a man who is supposed to represent the kindness and mercy of the Catholic faith. Ironically, the sadistic Father Dolan not only fails to hear the boy's "confession" of innocence, but he also oversteps his station by taking pleasure in paddling Stephen mercilessly in front of the class.

Momentarily, Stephen's faith seems to fail him, but he finds a solution to the injustice he has suffered in the chorus of classmates as they cry out in classical echoes of Roman crowds demanding democratic justice. Stephen's solution seems clear: he knows that he must visit the school's rector in order to clear his good name and report Father Dolan's injustice.

Stephen's surname, Dedalus, now becomes important in its relationship to his mythical counterpart, Daedalus. Like Daedalus, Stephen decides that the only means of escape from the tyranny of the school is to challenge the dark, labyrinthine corridors of the castle that lead toward the rector's office. Setting out, Stephen is anxious and self-conscious, convinced that the portraits of the saints on the walls of the corridor are looking down in judgment on him as he defies established tradition. They continue to stare as Stephen opens the refectory door.

What Stephen senses in the rector's office are strong life-and-death impressions, symbolic of Stephen's life-and-death anxiety about overstepping the authority of Father Dolan. As he confronts Father Conmee, the rector, the "solemn smell in the room" hints at the reverence of the occasion, and the skull on the desk portends Stephen's possible fate. But the rector's "kindlooking face" and pleasant manner encourage Stephen to state his problem boldly and with heroic simplicity: "I broke my glasses, sir."

Ultimately, the meeting proves successful, and Stephen feels comforted as he rushes down the gloomy corridors to the encouragement of his classmates. Realizing that he has fulfilled his quest, he feels like a celebrated hero returning from victorious battle. Democracy has prevailed. Carried aloft, airborne in his schoolmates' locked hands, Stephen views his world in a more amiable light: "The air was soft and grey and mild and evening was coming." This balance between light/dark, hot/cold imagery (not light, not dark, but grey; not hot, not cold, but mild) underscores Stephen's feelings of momentary contentment. Note, however, that Joyce says that "evening was coming." This is a hint that with wisdom, darkness will surely follow.

(Here and in the following chapters, difficult words and phrases, as well as Latin words and phrases are translated for you, as are those below.)

• **Et ignotas animum dimittit in artes.**   And he sent forth his spirit among the unknown arts. —Ovid, *Metamorphoses.*

• **looked at him through a glass**   looked at him through a monocle, an eyeglass for one eye.

• **put on the oilsheet**   put on an oilcloth, a cotton fabric made waterproof with oil and pigment; often used for tablecloths.

• **the sailor's hornpipe**   a lively dance, usually done by one person; popular with sailors.

• **Dante**   *not* Dante Alighieri. This is the nickname of the woman who is Stephen's nanny, or governess.

• **had two brushes in her press**   had two brushes in her closet—in this case, an upright piece of furniture used to hold clothes.

- **Michael Davitt**   Organizer of the land reform league. Much more of a political agitator than Parnell, Davitt served seven years in prison for attempting to send firearms into Ireland. He advocated nationalization of Irish lands and believed that Parnell was too moderate in his opposition to English rule.

- **Parnell**   Charles Stewart Parnell (1846-91); Irish Nationalist leader. Fought for Home Rule; urged Irish Catholics to pay no rents to their Protestant landlords. His political career was brought to an end when his adultery with a married woman was made public.

- **gave him a cachou**   gave him a cashew mint; often used for disguising bad breath.

- **the prefects**   teacher-supervisors; often senior pupils, as well, who are given authority to maintain discipline.

- **Kickham had greaves in his number**   Kickham had padded, protective shinguards in his locker, which was numbered for identification.

- **a hamper in the refectory**   a box, or basket of food in the dining hall that belongs to him; probably sent from home.

- **a magistrate**   a judge; to brag that one's father was a magistrate is to suggest that one is well-off, well-bred, and better than most.

- **never to peach on a fellow**   never to tattle or inform on someone else.

- **shortbread**   crisp, dry, buttery bars.

- **seventyseven to seventysix**   Stephen has 76 days until classes are dismissed for Christmas holidays.

- **the haha**   a sunken wall or barrier in a ditch, constructed to divide land without obstructing the landscape.

- **lights in the castle**   the "castle" refers to the complex that houses, among other things, the rector's quarters. The original castle, built in the medieval era, was destroyed in the seventeenth century and rebuilt. The Jesuits purchased it in 1814 and founded the prestigious Clongowes Wood College for boys.

- **shoulder him into the square ditch**   shove him into the cesspool.

- **Wells's seasoned hacking chestnut**   Wells's chestnut (used in a game); it has cracked (conquered) 40 others.

- **with her feet on the fender**   with her feet on a low metal guard before an open fireplace; a fender is used to deflect popping, or falling coals.

- **You are McGlade's suck.** You are McGlade's bootlicker, brown-noser, apple-polisher.

- **there were two cocks** there were two faucets — one marked "hot," the other "cold."

- **the hour for sums** the hour for arithmetic, or mathematics.

- **Go ahead, York! Go ahead, Lancaster!** the class is divided into two teams, each representing one of the two families (Lancaster, red rose; York, white rose) that battled for the English throne during the 40-year War of the Roses (1445-85). Shakespeare's *Henry VI, Parts 1,2,3* is set in this turbulent era and concerns its dynastic struggle for power.

- **he was not in a wax** he was not yet seethingly, passionately angry.

- **first place in elements** first place in the various required classes — Latin, mathematics, literature, and so forth.

- **two prints of butter** two pats of butter with patterned marks, or "prints" on top.

- **the clumsy scullion** the clumsy kitchen servant.

- **sick in your breadbasket** sick at the stomach.

- **knotting his false sleeves** Moonan is knotting two cloth streamers that are attached to the shoulders of the prefect's gown, or soutane.

- **he was in the third of grammar** he was an older student.

- **turned to the flyleaf** turned to the blank page in the front of the book.

- **do something for a cod** do something for a joke.

- **the seawall** a strong embankment to prevent the sea from coming up; a breakwater.

- **the kettle would be on the hob** the kettle would be on the shelf around the fireplace where families kept saucepans, teapots, matches, and so forth.

- **the fire of the smoking turf** turf is the name of blocks of peat which are cut from Irish bogs and burned for fuel.

- **getting up on the cars** competing with the railroads, these cars were long vehicles used for transport and were pulled by horses.

- **don't spy on us** another way of saying don't "peach" (or inform) on us.

- **not foxing** not pretending.

- **like the long back of a tramhorse** a tram was a horse-drawn passenger vehicle, much like a streetcar.

- **a dead mass** a mass said for someone who has died.

- **the catafalque** a raised structure on which a corpse is laid out for viewing.

- **a bowl of beeftea** a bowl of rich bouillon, or beef broth.

- **the liberator** usually the "l" is capitalized. The term refers to Daniel O'Connell who was, in 1775, Ireland's leading Catholic politician, advocating the right of Catholics to hold public office.

- **a green velvet mantle** a mantle is a loose, sleeveless cloak.

- **his feet resting on the toasted boss** his feet are resting by the fireplace on a very low, warm stool which has ornamental "ears," or bosses.

- **looked at himself in the pierglass** a pierglass is a tall mirror which fills the space between two windows.

- **a good breath of ozone round the Head** John and Simon have walked to Bray Head, a hill outside Bray, close to the sea.

- **went over to the sideboard** a piece of dining room furniture with shelves, doors, and drawers, used for holding tablecloths, linens, and silverware.

- **moisty and watery about the dewlaps** dewlaps refer to the loose, wrinked skin under the throat.

- **that's the real Ally Daly** that's a first-class turkey, the best!

- **an answer to the canon** an answer to the clergy's condemnation of Parnell.

- **the pope's nose** the triangular-shaped "tail" of a chicken or a turkey, where the tail fathers are attached.

- **Billy with the lip** William J. Walsh, archbishop of Dublin; he worked in league with Parnell for land reform, but refused to give Parnell vocal or political support when the O'Shea scandal broke.

- **the tub of guts up in Armagh** Michael Logue, another archbishop who didn't, but probably could have, used his influence to dispel the general condemnation of Parnell. Reference is taken from *Hamlet.*

- **Lord Leitrim's coachman**   the reference here is to an Irish coachman who was more loyal to his English landlord than he was to his Irish compatriots who attempted to kill Lord Leitrim. A person who is labeled as "Lord Leitrim's coachman" would be a lackey, subservient to England and having no patriotism for Ireland.

- **renegade catholics**   those Catholics who desert their faith.

- **a spoiled nun**   a woman who, for whatever reason, has turned away from her calling to be a nun.

- **the trinkets and the chainies**   geegaws, cheap jewelry, and china dishes.

- **not long before the chief died**   not long before Parnell died.

- **a drunken old harridan**   a drunken old hag.

- **Mr. Fox**   the pseudonym used by Parnell when he wrote letters to Kitty O'Shea.

- **condemned to death as a whiteboy**   whiteboys were somewhat like eighteenth-century KKK members; they wore white garbs at night and threatened Protestant landlords who were raising rents inordinately.

- **the fenian movement**   inspired by the American Civil War, these Irish-Americans returned to Ireland to stage a revolt of their own. They were quickly and successfully put down.

- **Terence Bellew MacManus**   when the body of the exiled MacManus was returned to Ireland for burial, church officials protested his burial in hallowed ground.

- **old Paul Cullen**   another Irish archbishop who was anti-nationalist.

- **upsetting her napkinring**   a napkin ring is a ring of china, metal, or wood that holds a folded napkin.

- **They were caught near the Hill of Lyons.**   "They" refers to five students.

- **they had fecked cash**   they had stolen cash.

- **I know why they scut**   I know why they tried to escape. "Scut" is defined in the dictionary as the tail of a rabbit, held high while running. In America, the verb form "high-tail it" is similar in meaning to the verb "scut."

- **the press in the sacristy**   a closet (a large piece of furniture) in the room where the sacred vessels and vestments are kept.

- **the crimped surplices** stiffly folded, white linen gowns worn over priests' cassocks.

- **boatbearer** he who carries the container with the dry incense during mass.

- **censer** the vessel in which the incense is burned.

- **in the square** in the school bathroom.

- **smugging** perhaps a combination of "smuggling" (suggesting something done clandestinely) and "smug" (meaning, to "make pretty"); here, the term refers to the secret homosexual horseplay that five students were caught at, including Simon Moonan and "Lady" Boyle ("Tusker" Boyle).

- **a trail of bunting** a trail of festive streamers.

- ***The Calico Belly*** a satiric play on words. Julius Caesar wrote *De Bello Gallico* (The Gallic War), a work that is often taught in Latin classes.

- **how many ferulae you are to get** a ferule is a metal-tipped cane or rod used to punish children. Here, it refers to how many times the students will be struck.

- **they are going to be flogged** in this context, flogged refers to being whipped by a cane on the buttocks.

- **out with your bum** expose your buttocks.

- **they had stolen a monstrance** in the Roman Catholic Church, a monstrance is a receptacle in which the consecrated host is exposed for adoration.

- **the noun** *mare* *mare* is Latin for sea or ocean.

- **ablative singular** the case that contains the ending of the object of the preposition.

- **the mark of the spade** the potato has an incision where the shovel sliced into it.

- **Ad Majorem Dei Gloriam** To the Greater Glory of God. This is the motto of the Jesuit order; students are usually instructed to place the initials A.M.D.G. at the tops of all their papers.

- **Hamilton Rowan** an Irish Nationalist who escaped from his English captors and hid in Clongowes. He tossed his hat out to make the English believe that he had left the castle; the ruse was successful.

38

- **the green baize door**   the inner door is covered with soft, green woolen fabric.

- **gallnuts**   nutlike galls, or abnormal growths on trees.

CHAPTER II

Summary

The chapter opens with Stephen at home; he is spending the summer with his family, who have moved from Bray to Blackrock, about five miles southeast of Dublin. Stephen enjoys being with his father and his great-uncle, Uncle Charles. He begins each day observing Uncle Charles as the old man in his tall hat, humming Irish tunes, leaves the house, smoking his foul-smelling "black twist" of tobacco and making ready to perform his morning defecation ritual in the "arbour" (the outhouse).

After the ritual, Uncle Charles and Stephen take their usual daily walk through the town marketplace; their next stop is the park, where they meet, as usual, Mike Flynn, an old friend of Stephen's father's; Mike is training Stephen to be a runner. Flynn, according to Stephen's father, has put "some of the best runners of modern times through his hands." Stephen has noticed Mike's "flabby stubblecovered face . . . and long stained fingers through which he roll[ed] his cigarette"; he doubts his father's exaggerated endorsement of Mike's qualifications.

Returning from his workout, Stephen accompanies Uncle Charles to the chapel, where the old man prays. Stephen doesn't understand his uncle's serious piety and wonders why his uncle is praying so fervently.

On weekends, Stephen takes long walks with his father and Uncle Charles, listening patiently to family stories and their conversations about Irish politics. Although Stephen fails to understand the meanings of some of their grown-up words, he has begun to find pleasure in the adventurous and romantic language of *The Count of Monte Cristo*. Reading the novel, he is transformed into the dark and dashing lover of the beautiful and modest Mercedes; with his friend Aubrey Mills, Stephen reenacts numerous battles and deeds of daring which help satisfy his boyhood appetite for a life of romance and adventure.

At the close of summer, Stephen learns that he will not be returning to Clongowes Wood College because of his father's mounting debts. Shortly thereafter, Stephen and his family move to a "cheerless house" in Dublin; there, Stephen realizes that his father is a financial failure. He becomes self-conscious and bitter, embarrassed by the squalid "change of fortune" which painfully affects his life.

In order to escape his unhappiness, Stephen immerses himself in fantasies of love and romance. Thoughts of the beautiful Mercedes merge with his loving memories of a certain girl; he attempts to calm his young storm of emotions by writing a poem to his beloved, "To E− C−." In an artistic re-creation of a meeting with this girl, Stephen composes a poem to her in romantic, Byronesque language. Afterward, he yearns even more for the girl, puzzling over his undefined ache for satisfying physical love−which, of course, he has not yet experienced.

When Stephen learns that his father has arranged for him to attend Belvedere College, a prestigious Jesuit day school, he is humiliated to learn that his father discussed the Clongowes pandying incident with Father Conmee *and* with Father Dolan. To Stephen's shame and dismay, they all "had a hearty laugh together" over Stephen's anguished confrontation with Father Conmee.

The next scene opens about two and a half years later. Stephen is probably fourteen years old, a confident young man at Belvedere, preparing to go onstage in the school play. During his years at Belvedere, Stephen has distinguished himself as an accomplished essay writer, actor, and model student.

Listening for his cue, Stephen waits outside the theater and is confronted by two classmates, Heron and Wallis, who propose a schoolboy prank. They mock Stephen's seriousness as a "model youth" and tease him about a girl who has shown interest in Stephen's upcoming performance in the play. Stephen answers their taunts irreverently; he rotely recites the *Confiteor* (the Roman Catholic prayer said during Mass for the confession of sin), and he recalls an earlier incident when Heron taunted him and initiated a similar response.

Stephen remembers his first year at Belvedere; it was a time when he felt terribly insecure about his home life and his future. He had begun to take pride in the success of his essay writing when Mr. Tate, the English teacher, discussed one of Stephen's essays, saying that it contained heresy. Strangely, Stephen felt a "vague . . . malignant joy" at being singled out by Mr. Tate. Afterward, Heron and two other troublesome classmates, apparently jealous of Stephen, confronted him and instigated a fight; during the incident, Stephen was forced to identify Cardinal Newman as his favorite prose writer and Byron as his favorite poet. The bullies – Heron, Boland, and Nash – all preferred Tennyson to the "heretical and immoral" Byron, and they attempted to force Stephen to "admit that Byron was no good" by beating Stephen until he finally freed himself. In spite of everything, though, Stephen remembers following after them, half-blinded by tears.

The memory is still vivid, but Stephen no longer bears the boys any malice; Stephen's former anger has been erased by his adolescent love for the young girl who has come to see him in the play. Her admiration for him far outweighs the boys' taunts.

Stephen's role in the play is that of a "farcical pedagogue," and he is somewhat embarrassed when he thinks about the girl viewing his schoolboy performance; as a result, after he finishes his lines, he rushes off the stage, past the audience and his family. He is confused, floundering in a sea of "wounded pride . . . fallen hope . . . and baffled desire."

We next see Stephen traveling with his father on a train toward Cork, where Simon plans to sell the remainder of his property at auction. Bored and disinterested during the train ride, Stephen observes his father – drinking from a flask and crying, on occasion, as he reminisces; he broodingly tells Stephen about old times and lost friends. Arriving at Simon's Alma Mater, Queen's College, Stephen watches as a porter humors his father, who continues his tiresome, endless tales about times past.

When at last they arrive at the anatomy theater, where Simon once studied as a medical student, Simon and the porter search for Simon's desk. Stephen lingers behind momentarily and is stunned to look down and see the word *Foetus* carved deeply into a desktop. Simon is describing his college days, but Stephen hears only words. Phantoms stand around him, laughing bawdily. Suddenly, he realizes that those young men long ago shared the "brutish . . . malady" of dark thoughts about sex that trouble Stephen. Until now, Stephen has believed that his preoccupation with sex is unique; now, these young men who carved the word *Foetus* into a desk during an anatomy lesson are linked with Stephen. He is not alone in imagining all sorts of dark fantasies.

Meanwhile, Simon is unaware of his son's anguish; he continues talking about old friends and gives Stephen scrap ends of advice. For example, he tells Stephen to always behave like a gentleman and to associate with students who have gentlemanly ways—the ability to sing songs, tell stories, and excel in athletics. The shallowness of Simon's advice and his admission that he doesn't really know how to be a father leaves Stephen feeling isolated, angry, and unsympathetic to his father's melodramatic and sentimental murmurings.

Stephen tries to escape from his feelings of alienation, but he can recall only memories of childhood experiences when he felt alienated, lonely and restless, as he does now. Meanwhile, Simon is still unaware of his son's sensitive turmoil, and he humiliates him when he and Stephen make a round of the local pubs.

Stephen's mind whirls, and his emotions intensify as he hears about his father's (and even his grandfather's) youthful flirtations and drunken revelries. Slowly, Stephen begins to emotionally detach himself from the pub crowd and resign himself to the fact that "his childhood was dead or lost and with it his soul . . ."

The next scene finds Stephen and his family waiting to claim the prize money for Stephen's winning essay. Excited at having so much money so suddenly, Stephen embarks on a lavish spending spree which includes dinners, gifts, and some redecoration of the Dedalus home. His elation in spending the prize money is surpassed only by his later feelings of shame as he realizes his foolishness in trying to "build a breakwater of order and elegance against the sordid tide of life."

Frustrated and disillusioned, Stephen dissociates himself from his family each evening. No longer a boy, Stephen wanders through the "dark slimy streets" of Dublin, trying to "appease the fierce longings of his heart," and, one night, feeling like a "baffled prowling beast," he arrives at the heart of Dublin's brothel district. Standing in a darkened doorway is a young, pink-gowned prostitute who invites Stephen to her room. It is here that Stephen is seduced into his first sexual experience; he "surrender[s] himself to her, body and mind . . ."

Commentary

Chapter II focuses on the end of Stephen's childhood and the beginning of his development as a young man. After his victory with the rector at Clongowes, Stephen begins to enjoy a relatively carefree summer with his family and friends at Blackrock. His happiness is soon shattered, however, by his family's financial ruin and the emotional confusion of early adolescence. Early in the chapter, we see that he still enjoys childhood's physical activities – playing, running, and enacting "adventures"; by the end of the chapter, he will have grown increasingly sullen as he learns more about the problems of the adult world. And he will have experienced sex with a prostitute.

This chapter, recording Stephen's emotions and thoughts from approximately eleven through fourteen, captures in detail the oscillating mood swings of an adolescent. Although this stage of development is difficult for any young person, Stephen's problems seem more intense – at least to him – because of his exaggerated sense of isolation, his romantic idealism, and his instinctive curiosity about all aspects of life.

On the verge of maturity, Stephen seeks an answer to the matter of manhood: what defines a man? His only role model is his pathetic father, Simon Dedalus. Simon tries to appear capable of caring for his family, but Stephen realizes that his father is a careless wastrel, responsible only for his family's increasing poverty.

The family's move to a cheerless, foggy section of Dublin causes Stephen painful disappointment and humiliation. Joyce understands the misery which Stephen suffers. He graphically describes Stephen's first night in the Dedaluses' new home, where "the parlor fire would not draw" . . . and the "half furnished uncarpeted room" was bathed in a "weak light over the boarded floor." Both the "gloomy foggy city" and the "bare cheerless house" make Stephen's "heart heavy" with the "intuition and foreknowledge" that it is his father who is responsible for the decline. To Stephen, the future seems hopeless. He knows that he is a bright young man and that he is possibly talented, but how does one rise above a future destined for the poor house?

Stephen's only escape from these harsh new surroundings is in wandering Dublin's streets and immersing himself in romantic reveries and fantasies. He is fascinated by his new freedom and the strange wildness of the city, but he is confused by his new and sudden arousals of sexual desire. The surging of sexual lust disturbs him because it seemingly conflicts with his chaste ideal of romantic love. He attempts to re-create a satisfactory solution in his verse-inspired daydream of the elusive E– C–, but fails. Stephen is a sexually maturing adolescent—confused, unhappy, and torn with strong feeling of restless alienation.

In addition to developing the theme of a young artist's feelings of alienation, Joyce also stresses the theme of betrayal—particularly in Stephen's relationship with his father. Simon Dedalus, although he fails to meet his family's financial needs, is extremely concerned with providing a quality education for his children. Stephen's father disappoints Stephen, however, because Simon and the other men laugh about Stephen's confrontation with Father Conmee—a triumphant moment in Stephen's young life, not something to have a "hearty laugh" about. Stephen feels dishonored and patronized by his elders. He particularly takes his father's betrayal to heart, and, years later, he will discover that he cannot forgive his father when Simon needs his son's sympathy and emotional support.

Although Joyce reveals only a few details about Stephen's first two years at Belvedere, we can assume that Stephen devoted much of his time to overcompensating academically in order to hide his embarrassment about his family's poverty. We know that at Belvedere, Stephen was praised for his writing ability and that he took secret pride in shocking his readers. We also know that he was a school leader and earned an important role in the school play. Nevertheless, in spite of all his accomplishments, Stephen remains tormented by his "soul's incurable loneliness," and he becomes increasingly desperate to find an outlet for his deeply troubling, restless emotions.

In the midst of his turmoil, Stephen accompanies his father when Simon must oversee the distasteful task of liquidating the remainder of the family estate. When Stephen and Simon visit Queen's College, Simon attempts to impress his son with old memories of his Alma Mater, but Stephen is unable to share any kind of emotional empathy. When he sees the word *Foetus* carved deeply on a desk top, he realizes, with shocked revulsion, that students of another generation experienced the same kind of dark thoughts that trouble him today.

Later, Stephen is repulsed by his father's behavior in one of the neighborhood bars. Simon is determined to make a vulgar display of his long-gone, swashbuckling virility. Stephen wonders if he himself will inherit his father's depravity; he fears that the only hope for any normalcy in his life lies in the possibility of foster parentage. This pathos of a father-son relationship during the visit to Cork initiates

Stephen's comment that paternity is little more than a "legal fiction."

The visit to Cork also reveals the irony in Joyce's use of the Daedalus myth. The mythical Daedalus, unlike Simon, was a capable, devoted father to his son, Icarus, and was genuinely concerned about the boy's future. In contrast, Simon has always rebelled against most of his paternal responsibilities, and, as a result, he has remained superficial and ineffectual in his fatherly role. Daedalus ultimately attempted to impart valuable advice regarding the ways of the world to his son, but Simon has failed to do this. His selfish sentimentality has driven Stephen further into his own moral and emotional morass.

The chapter concludes as Stephen, having failed to form a bond with his father, succumbs to sex: he will find warmth and comfort by giving himself over to the sexual emotions which have been consuming him. Although he longs to escape the filth and poverty of Dublin and launch out into a pursuit of pure truth, beauty, and love, his quest takes a detour in a short-lived moment of physical gratification in the welcoming, seductive arms of a young Dublin prostitute.

This pink-clad young woman provides Stephen with his first sexual experience, and she also symbolically resolves several of Stephen's emotional conflicts in regard to women. Thus far, women have been either saints, martyrs, or sinners to Stephen. Repeatedly Stephen has had to "apologise . . . admit . . . [and] confess" that he is attracted to women; these words imply that there is something wrong with his being attracted to women. In his early relationships with women, he has always felt suffocated with unresolved guilt and, as a result, he has developed an iron-like repression of his natural sexual impulses. This guilt about his feeling attracted to women has been compounded by his personal feelings about his mother, Dante, the Blessed Virgin, and Eileen. The Dublin prostitute embodies characteristics of all these women: she is youthful in appearance (she wears a pink dress and has a doll by the bed), yet she is confident and maternal (she nurtures him firmly and calms his fears by calling him a "little rascal"), and, as a result, Stephen, the young artist, worships her physically and spiritually during his immersion in sex, an act which is considered by some people to be the ultimate act of creation.

- **black twist**   coarse, black tobacco leaves twisted together.

- **outhouse**   outdoor toilet.

- **did messages**   delivered messages.

- **grandnephew**   great-nephew; Uncle Charles is Stephen's great-uncle.

- **took their constitutional**   they regularly took a walk for health's sake.

- **Munster**   Simon Dedalus' family home is in Cork, county of Munster, which was traditionally a political hotbed of deep national pride.

- *The Count of Monte Cristo*   a nineteenth-century novel about a handsome hero, Edmond Dantes, who is about to be married to his beautiful and beloved Mercedes when he is falsely accused of treason and imprisoned for fourteen years. He arranges a highly unlikely but melodramatically thrilling escape; then he unearths a treasure which finances several ingenious schemes of revenge on the men responsible for his imprisonment. The multiple allusions to Mercedes, Marseilles, sunny trellises, and moonlit gardens all refer to this novel.

- **Madam, I never eat muscatel grapes.**   Dantes (the Count of Monte Cristo) makes this statement to Mercedes; her son remarks that Dantes seems to have an Oriental code of honor – that is, he cannot eat or drink whatever is offered to him in his enemy's house. Because Mercedes married Dantes' rival, Fernand Mondego (alias Count de Morcerf), her house is technically the house of an enemy.

- **seawrack**   seaweed that has been cast up on shore.

- **gingernuts**   gingerbread.

- **railway carriage**   railway car.

- **quays**   piers lying alongside or projecting into the water for loading or unloading ships.

- **in search of Mercedes**   the reference is to Edmond Dantes' beloved, the heroine of *The Count of Monte Cristo.*

- **his stone of coal**   Irish unit of weight; 14 lbs.

- **the last tram**   trams were horse-drawn streetcars.

- **a new emerald exercise**   the reference is to unlined notebooks, similar to today's bluebooks.

- **A.M.D.G.**   *Ad Majorem Dei Gloriam* (To the Greater Glory of God), the motto of the Jesuit order; Stephen and his fellow students were instructed to place the initials A.M.D.G. at the tops of all their school exercises and essays.

- **his father's second moiety notices**   second half of the notices sent out in bankruptcy proceedings.

- **L.D.S.** *Laus Deo Semper* (Praise to God Always), another motto of the Jesuits; often placed at the top of the first page of a school exercise.

- **provincial of the order** head of a religious order in a province.

- **the christian brothers** The reference is to Dublin's Christian Brothers' School, an inexpensive day school for boys.

- **gamecocks** birds bred and especially fed for cock fighting.

- **Maurice** Stephen's brother.

- **the Whitsuntide play** refers to a play that is part of a ceremony commemorating Pentecost (the seventh Sunday after Easter).

- **stewards** ushers.

- **the Blessed Sacrament** the consecrated bread, or wafer.

- **Indian clubs** bottle-shaped clubs used in gymnastics.

- **singlets** undershirts.

- **Heron salaamed** Heron bent forward, in a low bow, his right palm on his forehead; this is an Arabic and Indian gesture of respect.

- **doesn't go to bazaars** Stephen doesn't go to large shops or flea markets selling unusually colorful and cheap, exotic items.

- **She's ripping, isn't she?** She's first-rate, splendid.

- **. . . that's one sure five** That's for sure; a top mark in billiards, using only one stroke.

- **the Confiteor** I confess; a formalized prayer said at the beginning of the Roman Catholic Mass.

- **had not forgotten a whit** he hadn't forgotten the tiniest detail about the incident.

- **in a great bake** another way of saying that someone is angry, or "hot under the collar."

- **his bally old play** "bally" is a euphemism for "bloody," which has no equivalent in American English; a "bloody shame" could roughly be translated as a "damned shame."

- **They drove in a jingle.** a jingle is a covered, two-wheeled Irish vehicle.

- **the boy who could sing a come-all-you**   the boy could sing popular pub songs.

- **drisheens**   a traditional Irish dish made of 1 pt. sheep's blood, 1 pt. milk, ½ pt. water, ½ pt. chopped mutton suet, 1 C. bread crumbs, salt, pepper, pinch of tansy, thyme leaves. The mixture is formed into a thick roll, tied tightly, and steamed for an hour. Good hot or chilled.

- **the anatomy theatre**   the room where anatomy was taught; usually a large room with seats in tiers.

- **legend**   here, the word means a carved inscription or caption.

- **Ay, bedad!**   Irish for "by God!"

- **some maneens like myself**   "maneens" is a Irish diminutive of men; Simon is being overly humble, a bit self-deprecating here in order to be well-liked.

- **slim jim**   long strips of candy.

- **the rector in a black and gold cope**   a "cope" is a form of "cloak"; it is long and is worn in processions.

- **beggars who importuned him for a lob**   beggars asking for only a small coin.

- **he was only a Dublin jakeen**   a snooty, lower-class Dubliner.

- **Tempora mutantur nos et mutamur in illis . . . Tempora mutantur et nos mutamur in illis.**   The times change us and we change in them . . . the times change and we change in them.

- **a fierce old fireeater**   a "fireeater" is a person who likes to argue and fight.

- **the quarter of the jews**   this is a misleading phrase. Stephen has actually wandered into the brothel district of Dublin.

CHAPTER III

Summary

In the days following Stephen's first sexual experience (Joyce refers to it as Stephen's "first violent sin"), he discovers that he craves food; his sexual appetite has seemingly whetted his appetite for meat and carrots and potatoes. His studies suddenly become either wholly unimportant—or else they take on new, shaming importance; for example, while completing a mathematical equation, Stephen is reminded that his sinful nature is increasingly multiplying.

Often Stephen feels slothful – lethargic, apathetic, and unable to pray. He feels that "a wave of vitality [has passed] out of him," taking with it his resistance to temptation. Although he knows that he is in danger of "eternal damnation," a "cold indifference" has seized him and prevents repentance and reparation.

Stephen feels contaminated by every kind of sin, but he continues to serve as the prefect of the Sodality of the Blessed Virgin Mary. The statue of the Virgin, the symbol of the "refuge of sinners," does not humiliate Stephen; he finds pity and comfort in the words of the litanies that he says in her honor.

Stephen also continues his catechism classes, but now he begins to contemplate the technicalities of religious doctrine that pertain to his "violent sin." He analyzes the origin and the result of his present sinful status, and he realizes that his sin of lust has rapidly spread into the other "deadly sin" categories – anger, covetousness, pride, envy, gluttony, and sloth. Then, at the very moment when Stephen is convinced that he has a consummately sinful nature, and when he is questioning the spiritual reality of the sacrament of the eucharist, he hears the rector announce the beginning of a three-day spiritual retreat which will be held at Belvedere in honor of the school's patron saint, Francis Xavier. The announcement of the retreat "wither[s] up" Stephen's heart.

On the first day of the retreat, Stephen sits on the front bench of the chapel as Father Arnall begins his sermon on the "last things" that happen to people –"death, judgment, hell and heaven." The gravity of this Judgment Day sermon, taken from Ecclesiasticus 7:36, penetrates Stephen's heart, making him vividly imagine the judgment that he would receive for the sin of lust – if he were to die suddenly. Father Arnall emphasizes that one should examine one's conscience and repent one's sins *while one still has the chance*. Stephen earnestly considers his pitiful state and the enormity of his offense against the omnipotent personality of God. His guilt increases, making him feel as though every word of the sermon is spoken personally to him.

Later, Stephen's thoughts turn to Emma (the girl about whom he fantasizes), the "packet of pictures" he hid, and the "foul long letters" which he left in a place where he was certain that some unknown girl would find them and read them. He shamefully entreats the

Blessed Virgin, who is less stern toward the sinner than God the Father, to understand his mistakes and have mercy on him – despite his terrible sins.

On the second day of the retreat, the sermon begins with these fearsome words from Isaiah 5:14: "Hell has enlarged its soul and opened its mouth without any limits." In other words, Hell has not yet gorged itself. Hell is still hungry – hungry for Stephen.

Stephen hears how God's once-beloved angel Lucifer, because of his pride, was hurled into the everlasting darkness of Hell by a vengeful God. Lucifer's sin was his refusal to serve God (*non serviam*). In order to fill the seats left vacant by Lucifer and his cohorts, God created Adam and Eve, but even they failed to obey His commands. Thus began the "inheritance" of mankind's sinful nature.

The retreat master reminds the boys that they were redeemed from Original Sin (their inherited sinful nature) by the death of Jesus Christ, who suffered crucifixion for the remission of the sins of the world. However, this reminder of God's supreme sacrifice of His son fails to comfort Stephen; instead, it causes him to grow increasingly remorseful as the speaker depicts ever more vividly the dark, burning punishments of Hell.

These graphic descriptions of Hell – its stench and its torments – are extremely painful for Stephen because the retreat master continually dwells on how the sinner will suffer through the *senses* – what the sinner will *hear,* what he will *smell,* what he will *see,* and the pain he will *feel.* Remember that despite Stephen's cold, rather contemptuous intellectuality, he has, since the beginning of this novel – ever since the moocow incident – perceived the world around him primarily in terms of his sensory awareness of it. Here, during Father Arnall's sermons, Stephen's deepest fears become frighteningly real. As he listens to the retreat master describe the crowded confinement of Hell, he can almost *feel* the bodies of the damned; as he imagines the smoky darkness of Hell, his eyes struggle to *see*; as he imagines the shrieking cacophony of Hell, his *ears* throb with pain; and as he imaginatively inhales the reeking inferno into which he will be cast for eternity because of his sins, the *smell* is overpowering.

But, Arnall emphasizes, the physical torture in Hell is only a *part* of eternal damnation; the psychological punishment will be as terrible as the physical punishment. He stresses that people who are consigned to Hell will have to endure the piercing, painful howls of the other damned sinners, as well as the jeers of the demons – all the while knowing that escape is impossible. Once a person is in Hell, there is no escape: he is there for eternity.

With his "legs shaking and the scalp of his head trembling as though it had been touched by ghostly fingers," Stephen leaves the chapel, horrified and guilty, fiercely aware of his need to be saved. Although he knows that he must make an immediate confession, he asks God to forgive his reluctance to do so in the college chapel because his shame is too great.

Later, after Father Arnall has discussed the physical existence of Hell in the first sermon and the physical and psychological torments in the second sermon, he begins his third sermon. Using Psalms 30:23 as an introduction, he describes the spiritual pain in Hell, focusing particularly on the *poena damni*, the pain of loss when one is removed from God's sight. Using bold, concrete imagery, he describes the cruel worm's (Satan's) "triple sting," the pain of conscience which causes the sinner to (1) remember his past pleasures with disgust, (2) see the "hideous malice" of the sin as God Himself sees it, and (3) realize that he deliberately chose *not* to repent and, therefore, must suffer damnation for eternity. The retreat master concludes by leading the congregation in an act of contrition.

Overwhelmed by the searing impact of the sermon, Stephen humbly returns to his room; he examines his conscience and, one by one, he calculates the magnitude of his sins. Later, as he climbs into bed, his imagination conjures up cruel, grotesque creatures, crowding around him in filthy, foul-smelling surroundings, swishing their long tails.

Shaken, Stephen flings back the blankets, absolutely convinced that God has given him this ominous vision in order to enable him to see "the hell [which was being] reserved for his sins."

Stephen vomits profusely "in agony," prays to the Blessed Virgin for help, and begins wandering through the "slimy" streets of Dublin in search of a remote church where some unknown priest can hear his confession. At a chapel on Church Street, he finds an old, kindly Capuchin cleric who listens lackadaisically, gives him his penance, and tells him platitudinously to ask the Blessed Virgin for help in overcoming temptation.

Relieved and elated, Stephen leaves the chapel in a state of grace.

Next morning, he takes Holy Communion during Mass and vows to begin a new life of purity and sanctity.

Commentary

Having committed the "violent" sin of lust, Stephen fears that he has initiated a chain reaction, what Thomas Aquinas called the Seven Deadly Sins. Stephen is aware of a "pride in himself," a pride in the "greatness" of his sin, a "covetousness in using money" to buy sexual favors from prostitutes, an "envy" of those whose vices are even more serious than his own, anger toward his innocent classmates, a "gluttonous enjoyment of his food," and a "spiritual and bodily sloth" which seems to have drained his whole being.

This obsession with sin causes Stephen to conjure up a series of "if's" and "why's" pertaining to religion. He tries to demystify his faith, challenge its validity, and perhaps find absolution through a religious technicality. Unhappily, the announcement of the retreat causes him to feel the full weight of his sin. He approaches the retreat experience with a "withered" heart and a feeling of dread.

The first and the briefest of the retreat sermons urges the boys to remember God's purpose for creating mankind; afterward, they should consider the present condition of their souls and then determine their fates if they were suddenly to die and have to face Divine Judgment. Would they go to Heaven? Or to Hell?

Clearly, this challenge of purity is difficult for a sixteen-year-old boy who enjoys sex and seeks out prostitutes as often as he can afford to do so; ironically, Stephen is viewed by the priests and the other boys as one of the "elder boys," a boy whose model behavior should be emulated by the younger boys. Throughout the first sermon, Stephen feels as though his spiritual life is passing before him, and, here, Joyce graphically records the details of Stephen's vivid imagination pertaining to his death and judgment. Stephen feels particularly agonized by Father Arnall's description of a lost soul because Stephen believes that he is *already* a lost soul. He believes that the sermon is delivered specifically to him—that he is being specifically warned about his sins: "Every word for him!"

At this point, Stephen begins to respond to life more intensely than ever in terms of his basic physical senses. Even after the sermon, Stephen continues to feel caged and tortured with guilt. He *hears* the "words of doom cried by the angel" and is mocked by the *sound* of a girl's laughter as he walks home from the retreat. In his mind, he *sees* the desecrated image of Emma, upon whose "innocence" he has "trampled"; the "sordid details of his orgies *stank* under his very nostrils." Next, he remembers *touching* the "sootcoated packet of pictures" and placing the "foul long letters" where a young girl can find them. Finally, he *tastes* tears on his lips as he imagines kissing the sleeve of the Blessed Virgin, imploring her to intervene and save his soul from eternal damnation.

Ellman's biography of Joyce suggests that there are parallels in Joyce's life with certain key features of this chapter. For example, Joyce's own sexual initiation occurred at a time when he himself was serving as prefect for the Sodality of the Blessed Virgin; later, Joyce possessed a perverse longing to "adore and desecrate" the one love of his life, Nora Barnacle. Joyce also wrote a series of "foul long letters" to Nora during their brief separation in 1909, but despite Nora's efforts to destroy these letters, Joyce hid some of them away, hoping that someday others might read them. Many people have read them; the letters offer keen insights and explanations for Joyce's literary treatment of women.

The second sermon of the retreat begins with an examination of the origin of sin — specifically, Lucifer's *prideful refusal to serve* God and obey His will. A description of Adam and Eve's fall from grace follows, and Christ's sacrifice is also detailed. The purpose of this spiritual exercise is to create the most terrifying vision imaginable of the physical torments of Hell and infuse the boys with anguished feelings of guilt and fear.

The priest intends to "put the fear of God" into these potentially wayward young boys. The "nature of that abode of the damned," as Joyce portrays it, dramatically reveals the underpinnings of Dante's *Inferno*. This coincidence is not surprising because Joyce revered Dante's masterpiece almost as much as he did the Bible; he considered Dante's works to be "spiritual food." Nonetheless, this particular Hell is very definitely a realm of Joyce's own design, wherein his fears of restriction and darkness are merged with residual anxieties from his early experiences with the Roman Catholic Church.

Joyce's personal hell is revealed through his emphasis on sensory details in this chapter. His poor vision required that he rely on his remaining senses; thus he emphasizes the stench and the taste of the air of Hell, filled with the toxins of "rotting human fungus," the interminable screams of the anguished sinners, and the "unspeakable fury" of the flames as they devour human flesh.

Joyce also understands the internal torment of the "company of the damned" and describes its lowly stature with vivid animal imagery: "a cock, a monkey and a serpent . . . hateful and hurtful beasts." This animal imagery, as well as the "goatish" beasts which haunt Stephen's dreams, is derived from our enormous stock of Western mythical lore and symbols.

The final sermon of the retreat climaxes in a series of questions from the "voices of conscience": "Why did you sin? . . . Why did you not give up . . . that impure habit? . . . Why did you not . . . repent of your evils ways?" Here, Stephen suffers a "spasm of religious terror" and is obsessed with a burning need to confess and begin a dedicated reparation of his life.

During the third sermon, Stephen contemplates the torment of a life without God. As the retreat master focuses on the darkness of an eternity removed from God's divine presence, Stephen imagines himself bearing the full burden of his sins until the end of time. Finally, as the retreat master examines the concept of eternity in a vast metaphor and concludes by discussing the grandeur of God, Stephen's "brain reel[s] dizzily" as he tries to fathom the enormous everlastingness of eternity.

During the past three days, Stephen has suffered terribly as he emotionally conjured up the burning torments of Hell. He has undergone physical anguish, as well as spiritual and imaginative Hell; his has been a journey that parallels the period of testing common to most mythical heroes. The mythical hero's descent into Hell is detailed in Dante's *Inferno*, and Daedalus, Stephen's mythical namesake, disobeyed orders from the powerful King Minos and was cast into the labyrinth of his own design, imprisoned with the monstrous Minotaur. Similarly, Stephen, through his disobedience to God's will, has been cast into a loathsome hell of his own imagination, where he suffers restriction and is threatened by beasts within his soul.

Stephen's repentance and humility is closely paralleled with the biblical story of the disobedient Jonah, who was confined in the belly of a whale. After three days and a humble repentance, Jonah was cast out of the whale. This duration of three days also carries the symbolic significance of the three days during which Christ descended into the depths of Hell and returned with the keys of Hell and Death; thus he atoned for man's sins and became his Redeemer. Stephen's three-day retreat enables him to imaginatively experience Hell, repent his sins, and fly free (like Daedalus) from damnation, through sincere and contrite confession.

It is worth noting that although the chapter concludes with Stephen's confession and rededication to a life without sin, the Capuchin priest was chosen by Stephen because he believed that the Capuchin would be more merciful in his directives than Stephen's own priest would have been at Belvedere College. Note, too, that Stephen shows his preference for the benignity of Mary, rather than confront the stern justice of an omnipotent male God. Even the act of confessing to a Capuchin priest ("capuchin" also means a hooded cloak worn by women), rather than a possibly "tough" priest at Belvedere College, indicates Stephen's growing tendency toward creating a softer, more beautiful world to exist in, rather than enduring the harsh, more realistic one.

• **his scribbler**   his notebook.

• **Shelley's fragment**   the reference is to Shelley's unfinished poem "To the Moon."

• **sinned mortally**   to commit a mortal sin, one must be fully aware that a sin is being committed; knowingly and willingly acting against the laws of God.

• **grace**   the freely given, unmerited favor and love of God; the condition of being in God's favor.

• **surd**   an irrational number; the root of an integer.

• **Sodality of the Blessed Virgin Mary**   a religious association formed by the Jesuit order and based on Loyola's devotion to the Blessed Virgin Mary. Stephen is the administrative leader (prefect) of this organization, which performs charitable works and meets on Saturday mornings for prayers in honor of the Virgin Mary.

• **Quasi cedrus exalta sum . . . odoris.**   I was exalted just as the cedars of Lebanon and the cypress trees of Mount Zion. I was exalted just as the palms in Cadiz (Spain) and as the roses in Jericho. I was exalted just as the beautiful olives on the plains and the plane trees that grow alongside the streams. Just as I gave forth the strong fragrance of cinnamon and the balsam tree, I also gave forth the sweet fragrance of the choicest myrrh.

- **sums and cuts**   the teacher has assigned the next problems to be done.

- **Ennis, who had gone to the yard**   Ennis had gone to the school urinal.

- **We can scut the whole hour.**   We have the next hour free.

- **catechism**   a series of questions and answers containing the summing up and the key principles of Catholicism.

- **the particular judgment**   this judgment occurs immediately following death; the Day of Final Judgment, the Last Judgment, occurs when Christ returns to earth and pronounces the final destiny for those who are still alive.

- **Emma**   the reference is to Emma Clery, the young girl to whom Stephen has written poems, much as Dante did to Beatrice.

- **hanged upon a gibbet**   a strange, seemingly vernacular description of the Crucifixion; perhaps Father Arnall is using the phrase to impress upon the boys the fact that Christ was executed "like a common criminal."

- **in a blue funk**   to be in a state of terror; in American slang, one could say that Father Arnall was trying to scare the boys out of their wits.

- **Saint Thomas**   Saint Thomas Aquinas; thirteenth-century monk, theologian, and philosopher. His works summarize all that is known about God by evidence of reasoning and faith and serve as the cornerstone of the Roman Catholic faith. Stephen develops his own aesthetic theory from the ideas of Aquinas and Aristotle.

- **venial sin**   a minor sin, committed without full understanding of its seriousness or without full consent of the will.

- **he repeated the act of contrition**   Stephen is repeating the traditional prayer of repentent sinners, vowing nevermore to sin.

- **his angel guardian**   every baptized Roman Catholic has a personal guardian angel.

- **the ciborium**   the container for the consecrated wafers.

- **Corpus Domini nostri**   the Body of our Lord; the words spoken before serving the Host, or wafer, during communion.

- **In vitam eternam. Amen.**   Into eternal life. So be it.

CHAPTER IV

Summary

The chapter opens with Stephen's dedicating himself to a life of "resolute piety," vowing to adhere rigidly to the rituals of the Catholic faith. Every day he attends early Mass, says rosaries on the beads which he carries in his trouser pockets, offers up supplications to remit the sins of those in Purgatory, and prays daily to be purged of the seven deadly sins.

In order to prove the sincerity of his renewed dedication to God, Stephen begins a series of mortifications of the flesh, trying his best to undo his sins of the past. "Each of his *senses* was brought under a rigorous discipline" (emphasis ours). He wakes early, endures the raw morning wind on his way to Mass, observes all Church-sanctioned fasts, and even attempts to sleep without movement in order to bring each of his senses under this new, harsh discipline.

As a result, Stephen begins to feel awe for the "august incomprehensibility" of the Trinity; he is similarly overwhelmed by his present state of grace and by the love which he believes God has for his soul. In time, however, old feelings – anger, willfulness, and desire – begin to creep under this new, amended facade. He begins to doubt the condition of his soul, and he fears that his soul might already have "fallen" without his knowledge.

Stephen's doubts increase. He wonders whether his hasty confession to the Capuchin was genuine or merely a reaction to Father Arnall's orchestration of terror. He searches for a sign that his "confession [was] good," then realizes with astonishment that the "surest sign" of a good confession is this fact: "I have amended my life, have I not?"

Coincidentally, the director of the school has taken notice of Stephen's fervent piety and invites him to his office to discuss the possibility of a religious vocation for Stephen. During the meeting, Stephen is puzzled; the director's tone reveals an almost flippant worldliness, and Stephen also discerns obvious attempts at manipulation.

Stephen confesses to the director that he has considered becoming a priest, and almost immediately, he begins to fantasize about the power he would possess if he were to join the clergy. The director's somber warning to consider the seriousness of "the call" ends the meeting, and they part with a handshake and an agreement to pray about Stephen's decision.

Afterward, Stephen considers the grim realities of the clerical life and the truth about his apparent inability to control troubling, emotional urges which continue to surface. As he recalls the restrictions of his years at Clongowes and Belvedere, his body seems instinctively to revolt against thoughts of living for the rest of his life in a confined community. He begins to realize that the basic weakness of his nature will inevitably lead him to "fall" and that his probable "destiny [is] to be elusive of social or religious orders."

Troubled by these truths while he is walking home, Stephen crosses the bridge over the Tolka River. Reflecting on his past, he looks back and sees the shrine of the Blessed Virgin; it seems to be a "faded" memory. Stephen turns and goes forward with an unburdened heart toward the "disorder, the misrule and confusion of his father's house."

At home, he learns from his sister that the family is moving again. Once more, Mr. Dedalus' mounting debts have dashed any hopes for stability in the Dedalus household. The young children attempt to make light of the situation by playing word games and singing songs, but Stephen notices that despite their gaiety, they all seem to be "weary of life." As he watches them, and even joins them briefly in song, he realizes that he deeply desires to be free—not only free from the religious life, but free from the hopelessness and the poverty of his family.

Walking seaward, Stephen feels oddly optimistic—perhaps his destiny is not doomed, after all. He is sure that he can find "better things" in life if he attends the university. He is troubled now only because he doesn't have a sense of direction for his life.

Shortly thereafter, a group of his friends playfully announce his arrival: "Here comes The Dedalus!" Stephen interprets this mild derision as a kind of prophesy, and impetuously he casts aside his uncertainties. He vows to be like his namesake—Daedalus, the "great artificer." He will soar above the religious and cultural restrictions of his past and fly toward a future of his own artistic freedom.

Realizing the importance of this revelation, he senses that he has left his boyhood behind. "Alone . . . unheeded . . . and near to the wild heart of life," Stephen moves toward the sea, where he sees a young girl standing in midstream, gazing out to sea, her skirts tucked up around her waist. Stephen studies her as she stands before him, and she returns his gaze. Silently, she gives him the answer he seeks.

This is a moment of epiphany for Stephen. He cries out "Heavenly God!" in "an outburst of profane joy." In this girl's image, Stephen realizes the importance of solitude in the appreciation of beauty. He can "worship" her as though she were an object of art, and he no longer has to feel shame because of his desire for her. She reveals to Stephen that his vocation, or his "call," is to live his life fully, regardless of error, and while doing so, "recreate life out of life!"

The chapter concludes as Stephen pauses to rest on the beach. He falls asleep and awakens much later, long after night has fallen.

Commentary

After his confession to the Capuchin, Stephen overcompensates for his sins of the past. He becomes a slave, as it were, to the rituals of the Catholic faith. He devotes all his free time to prayer and meditation. Imagining himself to be one of the first Christians "kneeling at mass in the catacombs," Stephen tries simultaneously to experience the privilege and the persecution of practicing his faith. However, by subjecting himself to continual self-denial and repeated physical discomforts, he seems more a sinner than a young, zealous Catholic. Moreover, his compulsion to fill his time continually with some form of devotion reveals a deep fear of allowing himself even one free moment – lest some minor, impulsive "weakness" manifest itself.

In this chapter, Joyce looks back on his own youth, and through Stephen, he "mocks his own religious revival a little." (Ellman) In particular, Joyce satirizes the compulsive, repetitive nature of the Roman Catholic faith. Stephen's obsessive observances of the mass, the rosaries, and the contemplation of each person of the Trinity makes him melodramatically aware of the "great mystery of love" which God has for him, *but* the discovery of this love is not comforting. It causes Stephen to mortify his flesh increasingly through ever more strict discipline of the senses.

As we have seen on several occasions, Stephen perceives the world through his senses; therefore, his mortification of his senses is a supreme sacrifice. Stephen is voluntarily relinquishing both the judgments and pleasures which he once derived from his sensual perceptions of the world. By shutting his eyes to diversions, enduring foul smells and harsh sounds, observing all fasts and controlling his physical movements in bed, he (like the mythical Daedalus) is creating a restrictive environment in which he is unwittingly imprisoning himself. It is almost inevitable that he will soon feel the urgency to escape this prison.

In spite of Stephen's valiant efforts to suppress his natural instincts, he is aware that his basic sensual self is reemerging. One by one – beginning with anger – his former "sinful" tendencies begin to surface, and, one by one, the "withered" layers of his forced spirituality begin to fall away. Feeling terrified and defenseless against growing temptations, Stephen seeks proof of salvation.

Instead of proof, though, Stephen finds only silence, and here is one of the key turning points of this chapter. Here is the advent of Stephen's *non serviam* credo.

The following scene, dealing with Stephen's possible religious vocation, is rich with religious allusions, all reflecting on the various themes of the novel. But before we discuss the specifics of the dialogue between Stephen and the director, we should point out a truism about many young Catholic boys and girls who attend conservative, parochial schools.

It is practically universal that students who have been schooled by church clergy or laity have, at least momentarily, considered a religious vocation. Some students are attracted by the power, others by the ritual, and still others by the unselfish devotion of missionary work. Consequently, when a teacher, priest, or nun notices the piety and dedication of a student like Stephen, that student is usually targeted for a talk about a religious vocation. Here, Joyce satirizes the so-called honor of being selected by a priest to discuss a "religious calling." Note also Joyce's elaborate use of religious imagery here.

The description of the director, as he stands in front of the illuminated backdrop of the window, makes him seem like an icon, or a saintly object of religious worship. Joyce soon reverses this image. When Stephen enters the room, he sees the director "leaning . . . on the crossblind." This image is a clever pun, indicating the director's actual, physical stance, as well as his intention to "lean on" Stephen about choosing a religious vocation – primarily because Stephen has been made temporarily "blind" by the "cross."

Note, too, the director's calculated smile as he "slowly dangl[es] and loop[s] the cord of the other blind"; Joyce makes the director seem like a skillful hangman, eagerly awaiting a chance to snare Stephen in his noose. In addition, the priest's face, in "a total shadow," raises the possibility of an underlying darkness in his nature, with the "deeply grooved temples and the curves of his skull" reminiscent of the skull which rested conspicuously on the rector's desk at Clongowes. Ultimately, this view of the priest causes readers (and possibly even Stephen) to wonder whether the cleric is really no more than a religious hangman who intends to make Stephen his next victim.

The conversation between Stephen and the director is less pious than Stephen imagined it would be. Instead of discussing profound matters of faith, the priest attempts to disarm the youth by speaking of his own school days and ridiculing the dress and manner of various, less worldly orders of the priesthood. When he discusses the long-robed Capuchins, he mocks them, referring to them as "Les jupes" (the skirts). Stephen is startled, even embarrassed, by the director's inappropriate comment.

This moment of insensitive ridicule reminds us of the time when Stephen's father laughed heartily with the Jesuit priests about Stephen's pandying incident at Clongowes. Here is another instance of Joyce's theme of betrayal by the father(s). Stephen has been betrayed by his own father (Simon), by Father Conmee, and Father Dolan. Now, this "father" has seemingly betrayed Stephen's concept of what a priest should be. Clearly, the director is not a man of discretion; he has revealed a worldliness that Stephen finds distasteful and inappropriate.

Throughout this scene, we can see a pattern emerging, linking significant events throughout the novel. Stephen is an unusually sensitive young man, and he is beginning to realize that anyone who expresses any measure of passionate concern (such as Parnell, Brother Michael, the Capuchins, and especially Stephen himself) is destined for betrayal by Ireland's proud and practical "fathers." This scene, focusing on the theme of betrayal, prepares us for Stephen's impending decision to choose a new kind of life for himself.

Stephen compares his childhood perceptions of the priesthood with his present, more discerning viewpoint: "Lately, some of their judgements had sounded a little childish in his ears and had made him feel a regret and pity. . ." He leaves the meeting with a feeling of "unresting doubt" about a religious vocation.

At this point, we have little doubt about Stephen's final decision regarding a religious vocation. Joyce's diction reveals the conclusion of the matter. Note his description of the "grave and ordered . . . passionless" life from which Stephen turns as he crosses the bridge over the Tolka and "descend[s]" into the disorder of the natural world.

When Stephen turns on the bridge and looks back, symbolically he is choosing between his mother's religiously restricted world (his mother's name is Mary, the same as the name of the Blessed Virgin) and his father's irresponsible and reckless world. For the present, Stephen turns from religion and enters his father's world, but eventually Stephen will reject the restrictions of *both* worlds, preferring to create a new and better life, one which offers more hope for his future.

Stephen decides that his new life should begin with his studying at the university. The possibility of limitless knowledge excites him to view the beauty of the day and enunciate his feelings about its beauty in a vivid arrangement of words that he retrieves from his memory lore: "A day of dappled seaborne clouds," he says. He realizes that the beauty of the day can be captured, contained, and painted in words. The artist in Stephen has once again surfaced.

Also simultaneously as he is "fabricating" his poetic vision, he is addressed by his friends as "Stephanos the Dedalos," and he realizes that his destiny lies with the spirit of his mythical namesake.

This scene intricately interweaves references to Daedalus and Icarus as they both relate to Stephen's experience of leaving adolescence behind and entering the adult world. Joyce refers to Stephen's hearing the "noise of the dim waves" calling him to freedom; he imagines that he can see a "winged form [Daedalus' son Icarus] flying . . . and climbing the air." This symbol from the Daedalus myth becomes clearer; it is a "hawklike man flying sunward above the sea." Then Joyce draws our attention to the fate of Icarus, and we hear the playful comments of one of Stephen's friends crying out: "O, cripes, I'm drowned!"

As the boys call out to Stephen, "Stephaneforos!" (*effero* in Latin means "to designate, or call forth by name"), the rebellious boy within Stephen dies (young Icarus drowns), and the great artist within Stephen (Daedalus) emerges. Joyce emphasizes the significance of this moment of death/birth by saying, "His soul had arisen from the grave of boyhood, spurning her graveclothes." This passage, reminiscent of Lazarus' and, specifically, of Christ's resurrection from the dead, is followed by a repeated affirmation of life, "Yes! Yes! Yes!" (words which Joyce reiterates in the final chapter of *Ulysses*). Stephen is announcing the new "freedom and power of his soul" which he intends to express through his life as an artist.

This moment of heightened emotion and artistic spirituality marks the climax of the novel, and Joyce provides Stephen with an accompanying epiphany. His description of a young woman standing in the sea is difficult for most readers to comprehend initially, but a careful examination of the imagery reveals the incredible impact of this experience on Stephen.

This scene is best understood if one views it as two separate scenes—first, we must realize that the girl is both an object of worship and an object of desire; second, the girl is a vehicle which compels the latent artist in Stephen to come forth. These two views overlay one another and effect Stephen's transition from adolescence into manhood.

The girl is a composite of the ideal female. We see her mythical significance as a "magic . . . strange and beautiful seabird," a bird that is also kin to the Daedalus myth. In addition, she is adorned with "emerald" (Irish) seaweed. For Stephen (the young, latent artist), she is both spiritual and intensely physical. She is "pure" and "ivory," and, at the same time, Stephen is keenly aware of her sexual allure, triggered by the sight of "the white fringes of her drawers." Stephen refers to her as a "darkplumaged dove"; this is an ideal oxymoron for this particular situation: doves are usually white, but this symbolic dove is dark, like Shakespeare's dark temptress.

Unlike the women whom Stephen has previously desired, this one accepts his worshipful desire and invites him to express his natural reaction of wonder. She encourages him by moving "her foot hither and thither" and, ultimately, she kindles Stephen's artistic nature by returning his gaze with the approval of the "faint flame . . . on her cheek." In Stephen's cry, "Heavenly God," he proclaims the "advent" of his life's purpose. He has discovered that he can see with the eyes of a man and, simultaneously, with the eyes of an artist. Afterward, he sleeps, awaiting the dawn of a new day and the dawn of his new life as a young artist.

- **ejaculation**   a short, sudden prayer or exclamation.

- **rosary**   a series of prayers (usually said with rosary beads) consisting of 15 decades (a group of 10) of aves, each decade being preceded by a Paternoster and followed by a Gloria Patri. One of the mysteries or events in the life of Christ or the Virgin Mary is recalled at each decade.

- **the three theological virtues** faith, hope, and charity.

- **Paraclete** another name for the Holy Ghost.

- **twigging** scraping a twig broom across a carpet.

- **foxpapered** discolored by age or mildew.

- **Inter ubera mea commorabitur** part of Song of Solomon (1:13), rendered in Latin. The entire verse reads: "My beloved is to me a bag of myrrh that lies between my breasts." Traditionally, the image suggests Christ's precious relation to the Church.

- **dominicans** a Catholic order founded by St. Dominic for the purpose of saving souls by preaching the gospel.

- **franciscans** a Catholic order founded by St. Francis for the purpose of imitating Christ's life of asceticism, coupled with a deep love of nature. Today, the order is associated with learning.

- **a muff** someone who's awkward at sports; here, Stephen is using the term to describe his youthful naivete at Clongowes.

- **thurible** a censer, where the incense is burned.

- **chasuble** a sleeveless, outer garment worn by the priest who celebrates the mass.

- **paten** the metal plate on which the bread is placed for the celebration of the Eucharist.

- **Ite, missa est** words spoken at the end of the Mass, meaning "Go, the Mass is ended."

- **the sin of Simon Magus** a magician who tried to persuade Peter and John to sell him the power to confer the spirit of the Holy Ghost.

- **a novena** a devotion consisting of prayers on nine consecutive days.

- **a stuff in the kisser** a punch in the face.

CHAPTER V

Summary

The final and longest chapter of the novel begins as Stephen sifts absently through pawn tickets that have provided money for the

Dedalus family to buy bare necessities. His mother chides him that he'll be late for class, and later she voices her fears that a university education will change him. Meanwhile, his father curses him for laziness. Feigning lightheartedness, Stephen bids them good-bye and is off to the world of the university.

In the next scene, we see that Stephen is not a model scholar. During an English literature lecture, for example, he is bored with the tedium of routine literary application. His mind wanders, making it impossible for him to concentrate. He attempts to escape the confinement of the uninspiring lecture by thinking about words — their arrangement, their Latin derivatives, and their use in poetry — and he wonders if he'll ever escape routine study and be able to "forge out an esthetic philosophy" of his own.

At present, Stephen's theory of aesthetics is still in the formative stage, as is his personality and his character. However, during this chapter, we will see elements of his past life falling away gradually as Stephen interacts with his friends and university teachers who bring out new aspects of his evolving "young artist" self. By comparing Stephen with each of the characters he meets and speaks with, we can see how his intellect, his attitudes, and his aesthetic philosophy begin to take on new depths. For example, when MacCann approaches Stephen on the way to class, he calls Stephen "antisocial"; unlike his "democrat[ic]" classmate, Stephen is unconcerned about "equality among all classes and sexes."

The next student we meet is Davin, a simple but intense "peasant student," who addresses Stephen by the familiar name of "Stevie." Although Stephen is fond of Davin and values his passion and his athletic ability, he feels that Davin's loyalty to "the sorrowful legend of Ireland" makes him something of a "dullwitted loyal serf" (to England) and to the dying cause of Irish nationalism. Davin's provincial speech and attitudes are a marked contrast to the new, experimental eloquence of Stephen's thoughts and expressions. This contrast is best illustrated in Davin's recollection of his encounter with a young peasant woman. Although his experience loosely parallels Stephen's encounter with the girl standing in the stream (both women beckoned the men "without guile"), Stephen's poetic account elevates his experience to the level of art. In contrast, Davin's narrative, filled with crude Irish idioms, reduces his encounter to a shameful reality which is ultimately reflected in the eyes of a brash flower girl who greets them on the street in "her ragged dress . . . damp coarse hair and hoydenish face."

As Stephen goes toward the lecture hall, he meets the Dean of Studies, who engages him in a discussion of aesthetics and the responsibility of the artist. Speaking to the dean metaphorically about the nature of artistic enlightenment, Stephen attributes his own thoughts on the matter to the ideas of Aristotle and Aquinas. The dean's limited, literal understanding of Stephen's theoretical discourse frustrates Stephen and ultimately makes him pity the "faithful servingman" who fulfills his occupation without possessing true knowledge.

Stephen's discussion with the dean concludes when the physics professor enters and attempts to teach a group of willful, inconsiderate students. Joyce's emphasis on the ineffectiveness of Ireland's educational system is the impetus of this scene.

Afterward, Stephen takes part in a spirited discussion among a group of his fellow students. Later, he meets Cranly, a friend who, like the others, wants to discuss MacCann's petition for disarmament and the promotion of world peace. Stephen becomes irritated at Cranly's questioning and his insistence that Stephen sign the petition.

Stephen uses this situation as an opportunity to exert his independent thinking on the matter, and while doing so, he impresses Temple, an emotional, melodramatic fellow student. Temple follows Stephen around like an eager disciple, fervently supporting Stephen's decision *not* to sign the petition. His fawning attachment to Stephen so aggravates Cranly that Cranly tells Stephen, ". . . curse him! . . . Don't talk to him at all . . . you might as well be talking . . . to a flaming chamberpot as talking to Temple."

Soon, Cranly and Stephen are joined by two other students, Lynch and Davin, who provide Stephen with another opportunity to enunciate his developing aesthetic philosophy. Later, during a hurling match, Davin shows concern for Stephen's growing isolation and his self-exalting pride; Davin urges him to embrace his Irish heritage: "Try to be one of us," he says. Stephen immediately rejects the suggestion and denounces Davin's dauntless patriotism and vows to "fly by those nets" of "nationality, language, and religion" which threaten to confine him.

Eventually, Stephen and Lynch separate from the group gathered to observe the hurling match, and Stephen further explains his theory of aesthetics to Lynch. He points out that although Aristotle did not provide definitions for pity and terror, he himself has defined both terms. He defines "pity" as the emotion that results when suffering is presented to—and shared by—a human sufferer. "Terror," on the other hand, is the emotion that results when a human sufferer is presented with—and shares—the cause of human suffering.

Lynch doesn't understand these definitions, so Stephen repeats them, explaining the difference between "static" art (an appreciation of beauty for its own sake) and "kinetic" art (that which brings about an emotional response). Stephen then provides a step-by-step explanation of his aesthetic theory.

He proposes that "since the good is what is desirable, and since the true and the beautiful are most persistently desired, then the true and the beautiful must be good." (Ellman) Although Stephen does admit that what is beautiful to one person may *not* be beautiful to another, he emphasizes that the universal beauty of an object can be appreciated in terms of its "integras" (wholeness), its "consonantia" (harmony), and its "claritas" (radiance). Ultimately, he explains, the moment an individual comprehends and appreciates these qualities of an object of art, its beauty provides the observer with a spiritual experience which has been referred to as "the enchantment of the heart."

Lynch is confused but entertained by Stephen's definition of art, and so Stephen continues to explain how an individual can tell the difference between inferior and superior art. The "lyrical form," he states, "is the simplest verbal gesture of an instant of emotion," related directly to the experience of the artist *himself.* "Epical form," he continues, is a step *away* from the lyrical and presents the artist's "image in . . . relation to himself and to others." (The words "to others" are the key to this form of art.) Finally, the "dramatic form" is the most superior of the three forms of art because the artist's personality becomes submerged completely—leaving *the work standing alone,* interacting with others who observe it. This form of art fills "every person with . . . a vital force," which exudes from the work of art itself.

Stephen concludes that the duty of the true artist is to stand back from his completed creation and remain "indifferent" to it, allowing it to live a life of its own.

Following this lengthy explanation, rain begins to fall, and Stephen and Lynch return to the library. Lynch continues to talk, but Stephen is oblivious to his friend because he (Stephen) has observed Emma Clery, the girl to whom he has been attracted for a long time. He makes no attempt to speak to her, but his mind is filled with wonder: How does she spend her days? What is she thinking? Does she have a "simple and wilful heart"?

Next morning, Stephen awakens refreshed and impassioned by his dream about Emma. Her image created in him "an enchantment of the heart," which inspires him to write an elaborate villanelle in her honor, and as he does so, he recalls the first verse he wrote for her – ten years ago. Stephen is also reminded of the many times that he has thought about her since their first encounter on the tram steps. His completed, six-stanza villanelle contains a multi-dimensional view of her: she is an object of Stephen's worship, as well as a "temptress" of his desire.

In the next scene, Stephen is once again on the library steps. He gazes intently at the birds flying overhead. He counts them, traces their movements, and hears their cries as they beckon him to follow and "leave for ever the house of prayer and prudence into which he had been born." His thoughts are interrupted by the voices of Cranly, Dixon, Temple, and others. They begin a quicksilver, random discussion of political and religious ideas, and the bickering eventually develops into a battle of insults between Temple and Cranly, revealing their dislike for one another – primarily because of their jealousy over Stephen's attentions.

Suddenly, Emma – the girl of Stephen's dream – passes by; like the birds, she seems to invite Stephen to leave his life at the university. Urgently, Stephen asks Cranly to step away from the crowd for a private conversation; he desperately wants Cranly's opinion on a family matter: Stephen's mother is pressuring him to make his "Easter duty" (confession and communion), but Stephen, having adopted his *non serviam* credo, refuses to do so. Cranly advises Stephen to make his Easter duty – to please his mother, even though Stephen no longer believes in the sacredness of the Church rituals. Stephen counters with a series of logical retorts and makes Cranly wonder how a young man so "supersaturated with . . . religion" can *dis*believe in the ceremonial rites of the Church.

Stephen confesses that he was once a *fervent* Roman Catholic – just as he was once a fervent disciple of his family and his country. But, having been disappointed, betrayed, and restricted by all of them, he now prefers to leave them all behind. He feels a deep need to declare his artistic, spiritual, and national independence. Stephen is sad that he and Cranly no longer view such matters in the same way, and his remorse is further compounded when he senses Cranly's anguished fear of being left behind. Nevertheless, claiming to fear nothing – not even an eternity in Hell – Stephen concludes his discussion by stating, "I will not serve that in which I no longer believe whether it call itself my home, my fatherland, or my church."

The final section of the novel consists of Stephen's diary entries as he prepares to leave Ireland. His first entry on March 20 reflects his last conversation with Cranly. The entries made during the following week reflect his feelings about leaving his friends, his family, his countrymen, and his religion. As the entry dates approach the time of departure, Stephen's entries become more hopeful. They reveal an increasing fascination for language, and they contain references to mythical characters. In the entry recorded the day before he leaves Ireland, Stephen writes about his mother's prayer that he will "learn . . . what the heart is and what it feels." It is here that Stephen announces his avowed intention "to forge in the smithy of my soul the uncreated conscience of my race."

Stephen's final entry in his diary, dated April 27, invokes his mythical namesake, Daedalus. He asks his "old father, old artificer" to assist him in the pursuit of his artistic future.

Commentary

This chapter, the longest and most intricately analytical section of the novel, examines the influences (family, country, and religion) which have shaped Stephen's life thus far. It shows Stephen stripping himself, layer by layer, of each of the confining shackles which restrict his maturing artistic soul.

Unlike previous sections of the novel, this chapter is written in a lyrical and fragmented, discursive style. It reveals Stephen's metamorphosis into an artist as he rambles from subject to subject in an attempt to resolve his conflicts, and it summarizes Stephen's experiences thus far. Finally, we see Stephen putting them into perspective before he liberates himself in order to pursue his future as an artist living abroad – free from family, country, and religion.

When the chapter begins, we see a parallel between the pile of pawn tickets and Stephen's pawning his integrity for a blind, unexamined loyalty to family, country, and religion. Stephen feels that his life has a profound purpose – ironic, really, in view of the pile of pawn tickets before him and his seemingly hopeless, humble beginnings. As he leaves for the university, his soul is battered by the sound of "his father's whistle, his mother's mutterings, and the screech of an unseen maniac" (a mad nun crying, "Jesus! O Jesus! Jesus!"). In this brief scene, Joyce gives life to the three forces which Stephen wants to free himself from – his family, his country, and his religion. We see Stephen's father's ever-demanding egotism (a symbol of family); we feel the oppression of Stephen's mother's continuous, submissive martyrdom (a symbol of country), and finally, we hear the irrational, lost call of a nun (a symbol of religion). Desperate to escape these three restraints which chain his restless soul to a subservient, doomed future, Stephen commits himself irrevocably to freedom, vowing to escape beyond the "echoes" of the voices which "threaten to humble the pride of his youth."

The word "pride" refers here to Stephen's pride in the knowledge which he has gained while studying the world's greatest philosophers and writers. Other voices, however, also threaten Stephen's emerging artistic soul – in particular, the voices of his fellow students at the university who represent the newest generation of Ireland's blind, unimaginative, subservient citizens.

MacCann, who urges Stephen to sign a petition for universal peace, represents the blind, ineffectual, and traitorous zeal of Irish patriotism. MacCann seems more concerned that Stephen pay lip service to the cause of world peace than believe in the cause itself. In contrast to MacCann, Stephen holds fast to his individuality, preferring his own goals rather than those of the unenlightened masses.

Stephen's friend Davin is a remnant of Ireland's provincial past. In both his speech and his actions, Davin represents the naive Irish populace who worship "the sorrowful legend of Ireland." Deep within Davin's eyes, Stephen sees the "terror of soul of a starving village" and perceives Davin's "rude imagination," which has been shaped by "the broken lights of Irish myth."

Discarding Davin (a symbol of Irish patriotism and culture), Stephen proceeds to challenge the sterile, "monkish" knowledge that he is receiving in the Irish institutions of higher learning. During his conversation with the Dean of Studies, Stephen reveals the marked difference between the "practical arts," which the dean represents, and the "liberal arts," which Stephen admires. Here, Joyce uses a "light" metaphor (the lamp symbolizing enlightenment). We see that Stephen's figurative approach to aesthetics is superior to the dean's limited, literal views on the subject. It is comic that Stephen's continued attempts to clarify his views further confuse the dean. Nonetheless, Stephen has an opportunity here to differentiate between his own aesthetic use of language, as opposed to the language that is used in the "literary tradition . . . of the marketplace"–that is, that which is taught by the dean. Stephen perceives the dean's scholastic limitations, and he pities him for his uninspired, but faithful service to his order. He realizes that a university education cannot adequately prepare someone like himself if he is to attain unique, individual, aesthetic ideals.

In order to further examine Stephen's ideas about art and the nature of the artist, Joyce creates a scene between Stephen and Lynch, using Lynch as a sounding board against which Stephen can enunciate his philosophy of aesthetics. The device is wooden and Stephen's pontificating sometimes seems ponderously dense, but clearly Stephen is as insistent about these aesthetic concepts as Father Arnall was about his concepts of sin and hell; the two scenes create a powerful contrapuntal balance within the last half of the novel.

However, it does seem strange that Stephen would choose to talk so earnestly and intimately with Lynch. Lynch's irreverence for Stephen's ideas, his crude remarks, and his childish pranks make him an unlikely confidant for Stephen's emerging philosophy of aesthetics. Thus we turn to Ellman, Joyce's acclaimed biographer.

According to Ellman, Joyce had a reason for portraying Lynch as a lout: the reason was revenge. Joyce had a friend (Vincent Cosgrave) who continually mocked Joyce's serious dedication to literature; Cosgrave also interfered with some of Joyce's friendships, and once, he even tried to steal away Joyce's only love, Nora Barnacle. Thus, Joyce devised an opportunity to even the score with Cosgrave by creating an obnoxious, "reptilelike" character with a "shriveled soul" and an ominous name, Lynch. Lynch's buffoonery and crude language, used as a measure for comparison here, serve to elevate Stephen's esoteric views on beauty and art. In contrast to the low-class, scatological Lynch, Stephen emerges as a philosopher and artist who has confidently left Lynch behind to wallow in the "excrement[al]" meanderings of his shallow, rutted thoughts.

Another shackle which threatens Stephen's artistic freedom is his complex perception of women. The reappearance of Emma Clery, the object of Stephen's first verse (written more than ten years ago), inspires him to write a villanelle, which incorporates all of his conflicting emotions concerning women – his worship of them, his desecration of them, and his need to feel fulfilled by them. By recreating his feelings about Emma and women in general, using the artistic form of the villanelle, Stephen frees himself from a sexual compulsion for women and is rewarded for his efforts by a vision of birds, soaring freely and prophetically through the sky.

As Stephen contemplates the flight of the birds, he considers the mythic possibilities of his future. He wonders about his namesake, Daedalus, about the Egyptian god of the arts, "Thoth," and about his diminishing relationship with Ireland.

Perhaps the most important relationship which Stephen feels compelled to sever – if he is ever to leave family, faith, and country – is his deep-rooted friendship with Cranly. Cranly is a character based on Joyce's real-life friend John Byrne. Cranly is the "priestlike" companion with "womanish eyes," who has proven himself a faithful and sincere friend of Stephen's during their years at the university. Stephen searches for reasons to dissolve their friendship because "if friendship exists, it impugns the quality of exile and of lonely heroism." (Ellman)

The first "reason" that Stephen "creates" for ending his friendship with Cranly occurs when Emma Clery makes a bow "across Stephen" in reply to Cranly's greeting. To Stephen, the bow is metaphorical: has Cranly been dating Emma "behind Stephen's back"? Is this the explanation for Cranly's recent, aggressive behavior toward Stephen? Seeing Cranly's behavior as part of a pattern of betrayal, Stephen convinces himself that he has been betrayed by Cranly. Until now, Cranly has been Stephen's priest-like confidant, but now, just before leaving Ireland, Stephen can, if he chooses, use this moment to justify breaking off his friendship with Cranly.

At this point, Stephen overlooks Cranly's so-called betrayal. Later, when he asks Cranly's advice, he is pained to discover that Cranly seems to have no integrity. Cranly is firm: Stephen should honor his mother's request and perform his "Easter duty"– even though Stephen no longer believes in Catholic rituals. To Stephen, Cranly is the epitome of compromise. Just as Ireland has long compromised its people to England and to the superstitious Catholic Church, so Cranly would compromise principles. Stephen wants – and needs – to escape this polluted system of values. Thus Stephen announces his imminent departure, stating he has no fear that he is making a mistake by fleeing Ireland. He says that he is willing to suffer for his art, even if it means that he will suffer during eternity.

This final conversation between Stephen and Cranly is referred to in Stephen's diary, and it reflects similar entries in Joyce's own notebooks. In ungrammatical and fragmentary language, Stephen records his thoughts about Cranly and about Cranly's elderly parents; Stephen labels Cranly as a "child of exhausted loins." This reference, as well as the allusion to Elisabeth and Zachary on the entry of the following day, recalls the account found in Luke, Chapter 1, which records the story of the elderly Zechariah and his barren wife, Elisabeth, who, according to the announcement delivered by the angel Gabriel, eventually gave birth to John the Baptist, the anointed precursor of Jesus Christ. Just as John urged sinners to repent of their sins in order to be delivered from the wrath of God, so too does Cranly warn Stephen about his denial of faith. However, Stephen fails to heed his friend's warning and vows to pursue his artistic credo – even at the risk of damnation.

The subsequent entries in Stephen's diary similarly reveal his efforts to break his bonds with the past. The entry on April 15 is pertinent because we see Stephen contemplating Dante's chaste admiration for Beatrice. Again Stephen thinks about his last conversation with Emma Clery; however, this time, he does so with new insight. He says, "Yes, I liked her today . . . it seems a new feeling to me . . . O, give it up, old chap! Sleep it off!"

Is this new feeling akin to what MacCann suggested in his petition for sexual equality? Does this feeling mean that women can be viewed as persons as well as objects? Stephen doesn't know for sure. Remember that he is a young man who is – at present – somewhat incapable of discerning matters of the heart. Even his mother knows this fact, as we learn later.

On the day before Stephen's departure, his mother expresses her hope that his emotional development will eventually parallel his artistic idealism. She hopes that Stephen learns about matters of the heart – in particular, that human affection eventually becomes as important to Stephen as his ability to appreciate art.

At the end, Stephen acknowledges her wish, as well as the

possibilities that life has in store for him as he invokes his great patron's spirit to assist him on his way.

- **Gerhart Hauptman (1862-1946)**   a naturalist who treated serious subjects (such as alcoholism) in a raw, down-to-earth way.

- **Guido Cavalcanti**   Dante's fellow poet and friend.

- *Synopsis Philosophiae Scholasticae ad mentem divi Thomae*   Summary of the Philosophy and Academic Opinions of Saint Thomas.

- **hoardings**   board fence pasted up with lots of advertisements.

- **India mittit ebur**   India exports ivory.

- **Contrahit orator, variant in carmine vates.**   A speaker concludes; poets vary in their rhymings.

- **in tanto discrimine**   in so many disputes or separations.

- **the national poet of Ireland**   Thomas Moore (1779-1852)

- **a young fenian**   a young man who rejects his nation's serf-like relationship to England, believing so fervently in Irish independence that he is ready to embrace terrorism. Often, bands of fenians hid out in the hills.

- **a hurling match**   a game combining elements of field hockey and rugby.

- **camaun**   a piece of hurling equipment resembling a field hockey stick.

- **to redden my pipe**   to light it.

- **Vive l'Irelande!**   Long live Ireland!

- **the Ireland of Tone and Parnell**   the goal of these Irish Nationalists was self-rule, along with civil and religious toleration.

- **Pulcra sunt quae visa placent.**   That is beautiful which pleases one's sight; or, said another way, whatever pleases the observer is considered beautiful.

- **Bonum est in quod tendit appetitus.**   The good is that toward which the appetite tends.

- **Per aspera ad astra**   Through adversity to the stars. (After experiencing hardships, anything is possible; or, said another way, the sky's the limit!)

- **his ghostly father**   the priest to whom he confesses.

- **Kentish fire** a mighty show of applause, often stamping the feet, as well.

- **Ego habeo.** I have.

- **Quod?** What?

- **Per pax universalis** For universal peace.

- **Credo ut vos sanguinarius mendax estis . . . quia facies vostra monstrat ut vos in damno malo humore estis.** I believe that you are a bloody liar . . . because your face looks as though you're in a damned bad mood.

- **Quis est in malo humore . . . ego aut vos?** Which one [of us] is in a bad mood . . . I or you?

- **Pax super totum sanguinarium globum** Peace through the whole bloody world.

- **Nos ad manum ballum jocabimus.** Let's go play handball.

- **super spottum** on this very spot.

- **Pulcra sunt quae visa placent.** A thing is beautiful if the apprehension of it pleases.

- **visa** any form of aesthetic apprehension of perception, such as sight or hearing.

- **Pange lingua gloriosi.** Celebrate with a boastful tongue.

- **the Vexilla Regis** the royal or King's (standard) flag.

- **Goethe (1749-1832)** German playwright, poet, and novelist. His work is characterized by an interest in the natural, organic development of things, rather than in any dualistic schemes.

- *Laocoon* an essay by Gotthold Lessing, which is also known by the title, "On the Limits of Painting and Poetry." This dissertation disputes former theories on the subject and establishes Lessing's own differentiation between art criticism and literary criticism.

- *Turpin Hero* the old English ballad from which Joyce derived the title of an unfinished narrative, *Stephen Hero*, which eventually became *A Portrait*.

- **seraphim** the highest order of angels

- **a villanelle** a fixed nineteen-line form, originally a French invention, employing only two rhyming sounds and repeating the lines according to a set pattern. The finest villanelle in English is Dylan Thomas' "Do Not Go Gentle into That Good Night."

- **Ego credo ut vita pauperum est simpliciter atrox, simpliciter sanguinarius atrox, in Liverpoolio.** I believe that the life of the poor is simply atrocious, simply bloody atrocious, in Liverpool.

- **Thoth** the Egyptian god of wisdom and the inventor of the arts, sciences, and the system of hieroglyphics. The Greeks and Romans referred to him as the cunning communicator Hermes, or Mercury.

- **the opening of the national theatre** the production that night was *The Countess Cathleen.* The Catholics hated it, thought that it was blasphemous.

- *The Tablet* an ultra right-wing English Catholic paper.

- *The Bride of Lammermoor* one of Sir Walter Scott's most popular historical romances.

- **Pernobilis et pervetusta familia** an illustrious and old family ancestry.

- **paulo post futurum** it's going to be a little later.

- **ipso facto** obviously; as one can see; it speaks for itself.

- **Mulier cantat.** A woman is singing.

- **Et tu cum Jesu Galilaeo eras.** And you were with Jesus the Galilean.

- **risotto alla bergamasca** a rice dish made with cheese and either a fish or chicken stock, prepared in the style of Bergamo, Italy.

CHARACTER ANALYSIS

STEPHEN DEDALUS

Stephen's earliest memories—intensely vivid and fragmented—are proof that from the first, he always viewed his world from an artist's perspective. Later, as a young man, Stephen retains his childlike curiosity about people and things. He continues to make keen observations and displays an acute sensitivity which eventually causes him to realize that his destiny is to create—to become an artist and to define his artistic soul. Thus, he leaves for the Continent, severing himself from his family, his faith, and his country.

Stephen's journey through life, prior to his leaving for the Continent, is not easy. He is a troubled little boy, and it is little wonder. From his mother, Mary Joyce, while he is learning about piety, he takes on her deeply guilt-ridden sense of duty. In contrast, Stephen's father, Simon, teaches him only the most superficial code of social conduct, advocating irresponsibility as a means of finding personal freedom. Thus, Stephen's earliest morality consists of a combination of his mother's admonition, "Apologise," and his father's advice, "Never . . . peach on a fellow." One parent tells him to confess and feel guilty; the other tells him to lie and feel no guilt. This paradoxical legacy is indeed heavy emotional baggage for Stephen who, at six years old, is sent out to face the world at Clongowes Wood College.

At this Jesuit boarding school, Stephen is quickly initiated into a life of cruelty, isolation, and injustice; he learns that escape is possible only through short-lived personal victories. Understandably, Stephen is overcome by homesickness, feelings of inadequacy, and actual physical illness, all of which alienate him from his fellow students. Most of Stephen's efforts to adapt to Clongowes result in humiliation; for example, he is mocked when he confesses that Yes, his mother kisses him. Floundering in guilt and confusion, his soul cries out: "Yes, his mother kisses him. Was that right?" If so, why is he teased?

Other things also confuse Stephen: should he spy on his fellow classmates and report their sacrilegious behavior? He could do so easily and with good conscience, and he could certainly "peach" on the boy who pushed him in the "square ditch." These and other confusing issues cause Stephen to constantly be on the defensive and to yearn for the comfortable security of home. Ironically, when Stephen is able to return home for the Christmas holidays, he realizes that home is not the harmonious haven that it once seemed to be.

After the Christmas Day battle royal, Stephen views his family differently. He sees the tyranny of religious zeal (embodied in Dante, his governess), and he also sees the cost of anti-clerical, political activism (embodied in Mr. Casey, his father's friend). The argument between Dante and Mr. Casey proves to Stephen that the adult world is as flawed and as cruel as his own small world. He is further disillusioned when he learns that the clerical community contains its own form of hypocritical cruelty. He realizes that if he is to obtain justice at Clongowes (regarding the pandying incident), he must relinquis] personal weakness, fly in the face of both custom and tradition, and be willing to stand alone and confront the dark, unknown forces of the world.

Stephen's later experiences at Belvedere College initiate him into the turbulent world of adolescence. At Belvedere, Stephen feels confused and ashamed of his family's poverty, yet he overcompensates for his feelings of inadequacy by excelling in both drama and writing. Furthermore, he finds an artistic outlet for his adolescent moodiness in his love for Romantic literature.

In spite of his attempts to adjust to the school and to the Church, Stephen exhibits the restlessness and unpredictable mood swings of the typical adolescent, compounded by feelings of inferiority and, most of all, by persistent feelings of sexual urgency. Eventually, these longings for sex are satisfied in the arms of a Dublin prostitute. This experience marks the end of Stephen's innocence and the beginning of his search for life's deeper meanings.

At this point, Stephen's struggles with his sex drive seem all the more painful because he serves as prefect of the Sodality of the Blessed Virgin and, therefore, he has an obligation to provide a good example for the younger boys at the school. Stephen's period of lust and frustration, however, is short-lived. After listening to Father Arnall's Judgment Day sermons, delivered during a three-day religious retreat, Stephen is so consumed with guilt and fear that he seeks out a kindly Capuchin monk to hear his confession. Afterward, he vows to purify his life.

Accordingly, he becomes a model saint of a young lad; but this phase is also short-lived. Stephen finally acknowledges his feelings of sexuality, and he also acknowledges his own moral imperfections, as well as the moral imperfections of people around him. He becomes cynical about those who profess to have a flawless faith and begins to use his intellect and logic in order to dissect spiritual matters.

The question of whether or not Stephen should pursue a life of spirituality is resolved once and for all after his meeting with the Jesuit director, who unwittingly reveals that a religious life would deny Stephen all pleasures of the natural world—a fate Stephen cannot imagine. His decision to turn from a religious vocation makes him realize that he is now free—free to pursue the pleasures of life through art.

To Stephen, artistic expression involves more than a casual appreciation of style or form; it involves a complete communion of body, mind, and spirit. Stephen experiences this "esthetic harmony" as he gazes at a girl wading in the sea; she epitomizes his expectations of life in the form of art, freedom, and sexuality. From this moment, Stephen dedicates himself to the pursuit of such a life.

Stephen chooses to forge his future by first testing his new philosophy against the established customs, mores, and restrictions of Dublin society. Almost systematically, he interacts with his family and his friends, and one by one, he dissociates himself from them, as well as from the values that they represent.

Although we might not agree that it is necessary for Stephen to break free of all the bonds which tie him to his disappointing and unfulfilled past, we acknowledge that he alone must make the decision about leaving Ireland. Note that as Stephen departs from his homeland, in search of himself, he seems to possess the confidence, the egocentrism, and a tentative hope for the future common to everyone who leaves home for the first time. Although it is clear that his life's lessons have only begun, we wish him well and hope that his future will hold him "forever in good stead."

CRITICAL ESSAYS

JOYCE'S USE OF IMAGERY

Although Joyce is frequently praised for his mastery of the "stream-of-consciousness" narrative technique, his distinctive use of imagery has contributed much to the artistic development of the twentieth-century novel. Specifically in *A Portrait*, he uses imagery to establish motifs, identify symbols, and provide thematic unity throughout the work.

Perhaps the most obvious use of imagery in the novel occurs during the novel's first few pages, with the introduction of the sensory details which shape Stephen's early life: wet versus dry; hot versus cold; and light versus dark – all images of dichotomy which reveal the forces which will affect Stephen's life as he matures. If we can understand this imagery, then we can better understand Stephen's reasons for deciding to leave Ireland.

The wet/dry imagery, for example, is symbolic of Stephen's *natural response* to the world versus a *learned response*. As a small child, Stephen learns that any expression of a natural inclination (such as wetting the bed) is labeled "wrong"; the wet sheets will be replaced by a dry, reinforcing "oilsheet"–and a swift, unpleasant correction for inappropriate behavior. Thus, wet things relate to natural responses and dry things relate to learned behavior.

Other examples of this wet/dry imagery include the wetness of the cesspool (the square ditch) that Stephen is shoved into and the illness which follows; likewise, the "flood" of adolescent sexual feelings which engulf Stephen in "wavelet[s]," causing him guilt and shame. Seemingly, "wet" is bad; "dry" is good.

A turning point in this pattern occurs when Stephen crosses the "trembling bridge" over the river Tolka. He leaves behind his dry, "withered" heart, as well as most of the remnants of his Catholicism. As he wades through "a long rivulet in the strand," he encounters a young girl, described as a "strange and beautiful seabird." She gazes at Stephen from the sea, and her invitation to the "wet" (natural) life enables Stephen to make a climactic choice concerning his destiny as an artist. Later, after Stephen has explained his aesthetic philosophy to Lynch, rain begins to fall; seemingly, the heavens approve of Stephen's theories about art, as well as his choice of art as a career.

The hot/cold imagery similarly affects Stephen. At the beginning of the novel, Stephen clearly prefers his mother's warm smell to that of his father. For Stephen, "hot" is symbolic of the intensity of physical affection (and, in some cases, sin); "cold," on the other hand, is symbolic of propriety, order, and chastity. Specific examples of this symbolism can be found in Stephen's memories: resting in his mother's warm lap, being cared for by the kindly Brother Michael (when Stephen is recovering from a fever), and receiving a heated embrace from the Dublin prostitute during his first sexual encounter.

In contrast, the cold, slimy water of the square ditch is evidence of the cruel reality of his changing life at school; in addition, Stephen initially experiences a "cold . . . indifference" when he thinks about the Belvedere retreat, and his vision-like worship of Eileen (the young Protestant girl) has coldly symbolic, touch-me-not overtones; her hands, pure and white, enable him to understand the references to the Tower of Ivory in an oft-repeated Church litany.

The last of this set of opposites is concerned with the light/dark dichotomy: light symbolizes knowledge (confidence), and dark symbolizes ignorance (terror). Numerous examples of this conflict pervade the novel. In an early scene, when Stephen says that he will marry a Protestant, he is threatened with blindness: "Put out his eyes/ Apologise." Stephen is terrorized without knowing why; seemingly, a good Catholic boy should remain ignorant about other faiths—and perhaps even of women. Stephen's natural fondness for Eileen is condemned. Stephen is only a boy, but his sensitive artist's nature realizes that he is going to grow up in a world where he will be forced to suppress his true feelings and conform to society's rules and threats.

Stephen's broken glasses are also part of this light/dark imagery. Without his glasses, Stephen sees the world as if it were a dark blur; figuratively blinded, he cannot learn. And yet he is unjustly punished for telling the truth about the reason for his "blindness." He quickly realizes the potential, dark (irrational) cruelty of the clergy. Further on in the novel, there are recurrent images of darkness in the streets of Dublin—for example, when Stephen makes his way to the brothel district. Here, we also see the darkness within Stephen's heart as he wanders willfully toward sin. Later on, the philosophical discussion about the lamp with the Dean of Studies (Chapter V) reveals the "blindness" of this cleric, compared with the illumination of Stephen's aesthetic thoughts.

A close reading of the novel will produce many more images within these patterns. Joyce's use of them is essential as he constructs his intricate thematic structure.

Another kind of imagery in the novel is made up of references to colors and names. Colors, as Joyce uses them, often indicate the political and religious forces which affect Stephen's life. Similarly, Joyce uses names to evoke various images—specifically those which imply animal qualities, providing clues to Stephen's relationships with people.

For an example of color imagery, note that Dante owns two velvet-backed brushes—one maroon, one green. The maroon brush symbolizes Michael Davitt, the pro-Catholic activist of the Irish Land League; the green-backed brush symbolizes Charles Stewart Parnell. Once, Parnell was Dante's political hero *par excellence*, but after the Church denounced him, she ripped the green cloth from the back of her brush. Other references to color include Stephen's desire to have a "green rose" (an expression of his creative nature), instead of a white one or a red one, symbols of his class's scholastic teams.

Another reference to color imagery can be seen in Lynch's use of the term "yellow insolence" (Chapter V); instead of using the word "bloody," Lynch uses the word "yellow," indicating a sickly, cowardly attitude toward life. The idea of a "bloody" natural lust for living would be appalling to Lynch. Lynch's name, literally, means "to hang"; he has a "long slender flattened skull . . . like a hooded reptile . . . with a reptilelike . . . gaze and a self-embittered . . . soul."

Like Lynch, Temple is also representative of his name. Temple considers himself "a believer in the power of the mind." He admires Stephen greatly for his "independent thinking," and he himself tries to "think" about the problems of the world.

Cranly, like his name (cranium, meaning "skull"), is Stephen's "priestlike" companion, to whom he confesses his deepest feelings. Note that several of Joyce's references also focus on Stephen's image of Cranly's "severed head"; Cranly's symbolic significance to Stephen is similar to that of John the Baptist (the "martyred Christ"). The name "Cranly" also reminds us of the skull on the rector's desk and Joyce's emphasis on the shadowy skull of the Jesuit director who queries Stephen about a religious vocation.

Concerning the other imagery in the novel, perhaps the most pervasive is the imagery that pertains to Stephen's exile, or, specifically, his "flight" from Ireland. The flight imagery begins as early as his first days at Clongowes, when Stephen's oppressed feelings are symbolized by "a heavy bird flying low through the grey light." Later, a greasy football soars "like a heavy bird" through the sky. At that time, flight from unhappiness seemed impossible for Stephen, but as the novel progresses and Stephen begins to formulate his artistic ideals, the notion of flight seems possible.

For example, in Chapter IV, after Stephen renounces the possibility of a religious vocation, he feels a "proud sovereignty" as he crosses over the Tolka and his name is called out by his classmates; this incident is followed by another allusion to flight. Later, the girl wading in the sea is described as "delicate as a crane," with the fringes of her drawers . . . like the featherings of soft white down"; her bosom is described as "the breast of some darkplumaged dove." Her presence in this moment of epiphany enables Stephen to choose art as his vocation.

Finally, note that when Stephen's friends call him, his name seems to carry a "prophecy"; he sees a "winged form flying above the waves and . . . climbing in the air." The image of this "hawklike man flying sunward" is at the heart of the flight motif. As Stephen realizes his life's purpose, he sees his "soul . . . soaring in the air." He yearns to cry out like an "eagle on high." He experiences "an instant of wild flight" and is "delivered" free from the bondage of his past. At the end of the novel, Stephen cries out to Daedalus, his "old father, old artificer," and prepares for his own flight to artistic freedom.

THE QUESTION OF AUTOBIOGRAPHY

The question of how much autobiographical material Joyce inserted into the fictional character of Stephen Dedalus has long been a matter of debate. Scholars and critics still produce evidence on both sides of the issue, but for the most part, the question has been largely resolved through the contributions of Richard Ellman, Joyce's definitive biographer, and Joyce's brother Stanislaus, who wrote his own book about Joyce, *My Brother's Keeper.*

Despite the countless similarities between Joyce's own childhood and that of Stephen Dedalus, Stanislaus Joyce makes it clear that "Stephen Dedalus is an imaginary, not a real, self-portrait." Significant details exist to verify this view, including Joyce's school records at Clongowes and Belvedere, as well as recorded interviews with several of Joyce's friends. Stanislaus points out that although Joyce "followed his own development closely, has been his own model and [has] chosen to use many incidents from his own experience . . . he has [also] transformed and invented many others."

One example of such invention is Joyce's portrait of Stephen as a physically weak, cowering and innocent "victim" at Clongowes. In contrast to this view of Stephen, Stanislaus remembers Joyce as a relatively well-adjusted student and "a good athlete," who won "a variety of cups for his prowess in hurdling and walking." He also recalls that Joyce was less isolated, less retentively bookish, and at times, less manageable than Stephen. In the Clongowes' Punishment Book, we find that Joyce, unlike Stephen, was never pandied mistakenly for an incident involving broken glasses, but the book does record that Joyce received at least two pandies for forgetting to bring a book to class, and on another occasion, he was pandied for using "vulgar language."

Other variances between Stephen and Joyce are found in Joyce's treatment of Stephen's friends, most of whom are clearly intellectually inferior to him. Stanislaus remembers, to the contrary, that Joyce's friends provided him with significant mental stimulation throughout his adolescent development.

Yet another difference between the creator and the creation exists in Joyce's relationship with his father. Ellman states, "In *A Portrait*, Stephen denies that Simon is in any real sense his father, but James himself had no doubt that he was in every way his father's son." In addition, Stanislaus recalls the Cork incident in the novel (where Stephen travels with Simon to Cork) and states that Joyce's feelings during that trip were quite different; unlike Stephen, who was disgusted by his father's visits to various pubs, Stanislaus emphasizes that "my brother's [James's] letters home at the time were written in a tone of amusement even when he described going from one bar to another."

Joyce's fictional representations of his friends at the university are just that—fictional. He changed many of their personalities, invented non-existent dialogues, and deliberately excluded significant individuals in the novel. Clearly, Stephen Dedalus is Joyce's fictional *persona*, whom he used to express his ideas about the lyrical, epical, and dramatic forms of literature.

In conclusion, in spite of the obvious autobiographical similarities, Stephen is a fictional representation of Joyce's art. Stephen exists, as does the novel, as an example of the author's "handiwork," behind which Joyce is "invisible, refined out of existence, indifferent . . ." and, probably if he had his way in the matter, is still standing concealed somewhere, "paring his nails."

REVIEW QUESTIONS AND ESSAY TOPICS

1. Identify the three major incidents which affect Stephen emotionally in Chapter I. Which incident do you think changes him most? Why?

2. Why is Parnell's death so important in the novel? Cite examples of several characters' reactions to it to support your answer.

3. Discuss Stephen's changing view of the clergy as he matures. Give supporting examples and cite specific scenes in the novel.

4. Trace the origin and development of Stephen's own *non serviam* credo. Using specific incidents in the novel, discuss the evolution of Stephen's non-conformist attitudes.

5. In Chapter IV, Stephen experiences an epiphany. What does he learn about his feelings toward women and about art? Do you think he really understands, or is he still as confused as ever? Explain your answer.

6. Look up the literary term *Bildungsroman* in the dictionary. Afterward, describe how this novel fits the meaning of the term. Have you read any other novels that can be classified similarly? If so, compare this novel with a similar novel.

7. Concerning the Clongowes pandying incident, write a persuasive letter to Father Conmee in defense of Stephen, composing your letter as though you were an eyewitness to the event. Provide logical, emotional, and ethical reasons why Stephen should be justly compensated in the matter.

8. Examine Stephen's personal relationships with the women, both real and imagined, in his life. Show what effect they have upon his emotional development.

9. Look up the definition of *satire* in the dictionary. Joyce admits using satire in creating the sermons that are delivered during Stephen's three-day retreat. Examine the sermons carefully and tell why certain words, phrases, and entire passages seem to be evidence of Joyce's use of satire.

10. Account for Stephen's change of personality from Chapter IV to Chapter V. Explain the circumstances which lead to the changes.

11. Look for evidence in the novel where Stephen compares himself with (or identifies with) other leaders who have been martyred. In particular, find instances when he compares himself with Parnell or with Christ.

12. Compare and contrast Stephen's relationship with his two friends Lynch and Cranly. Include references to their conversations and

physical descriptions and discuss the significance which each of the young men has on Stephen.

SELECTED BIBLIOGRAPHY

ANDERSON, CHESTER G. *James Joyce and His World.* London: Thames and Hudson, 1967.

BATES, RONALD. "The Correspondence of Birds to Things of the Intellect," *James Joyce Quarterly* 2 (1965): 281-89.

BEEBE, MAURICE. "Joyce and Stephen Dedalus: The Problem of Autobiography," *A James Joyce Miscellany.* 2nd. ed., Ed. Marvin Malanger. Carbondale: Southern Illinois University Press, 1959.

BENSTOCK, BERNARD AND THOMAS F. STALEY, EDS. *Approaches to Joyce's Portrait: Ten Essays.* Pennsylvania: University of Pittsburgh, 1976.

BRIVIC, SHELDON. "Joycean Psychology," *Works In Progress: Joyce Centenary Essays.* Ed. Richard F. Peterson. Illinois: Southern Illinois University Press, 1983.

DEMING, ROBERT H. *A Bibliography of James Joyce Studies.* Rev. and Enl., 2nd. ed. Reference Publications in Literature. Boston: G.K. Hall, 1977.

ELLMAN, RICHARD. *The Consciousness of Joyce.* New York: Oxford University Press, 1977.

_____. *James Joyce.* New York: Oxford University Press, 1982.

_____. *Selected Letters of James Joyce.* New York: The Viking Press, 1975.

GORMAN, HERBERT. *James Joyce.* New York: Farrar & Rinehart, 1939.

JOYCE, STANISLAUS. *My Brother's Keeper.* Ed. Richard Ellman. New York: The Viking Press; London: Faber and Faber, 1958.

KENNER, HUGH. "The *Portrait* in Perspective," *Dublin's Joyce.* Bloomington: Indiana University Press, 1956.

LEVIN, HARRY. *James Joyce: A Critical Introduction.* Rev. Ed. New York: New Directions, 1960.

MORSE, J. MITCHELL. *The Sympathetic Alien: James Joyce and Catholicism.* Washington Square: New York University Press, 1959.

MOSLEY, VIRGINIA D. *Joyce and the Bible.* DeKalb: Northern Illinois University Press, 1967.

TINDALL, WILLIAM YORK. *The Joyce Country.* University Park: Penn State University Press, 1960.

WRIGHT, DAVID G. *Characters of Joyce.* New Jersey: Barnes and Noble Books, 1983.

Your Guides to Successful Test Preparation.

Cliffs Test Preparation Guides

• *Complete* • *Concise* • *Functional* • *In-depth*

cient preparation means better test scores. Go with the experts and use
's *Test Preparation Guides*. They focus on helping you know what to expect
n each test, and their test-taking techniques have been proven in class-
m programs nationwide. Recommended for individual use or as a part
formal test preparation program.

sher's ISBN Prefix 0-8220

ISBN	Title	Price	Qty.	ISBN	Title	Price
2078-5	ACT	8.95		2044-0	Police Sergeant Exam	9.95
2069-6	CBEST	8.95		2047-5	Police Officer Exam	14.95
2056-4	CLAST	9.95		2049-1	Police Management Exam	17.95
2071-8	ELM Review	8.95		2076-9	Praxis I: PPST	9.95
2077-7	GED	11.95		2017-3	Praxis II: NTE Core Battery	14.95
2061-0	GMAT	9.95		2074-2	SAT*	9.95
2073-4	GRE	9.95		2325-3	SAT II*	14.95
2066-1	LSAT	9.95		2072-6	TASP	8.95
2046-7	MAT	12.95		2079-3	TOEFL w/cassettes	29.95
2033-5	Math Review	8.95		2080-7	TOEFL Adv. Prac. (w/cass.)	24.95
2048-3	MSAT	24.95		2034-3	Verbal Review	7.95
2020-3	Memory Power for Exams	5.95		2043-2	Writing Proficiency Exam	8.95

Prices subject to change without notice.

lable at your
ksellers, or send
form with your
k or money order
liffs Notes, Inc.,
Box 80728,
oln, NE 68501
://www.cliffs.com

☐ Money order ☐ Check payable to Cliffs Notes, Inc.

☐ Visa ☐ Mastercard Signature_____

Card no. _____ Exp. date_____

Signature _____

Name _____

Address _____

City _____ State_____ Zip_____

*GRE, MSAT, Praxis PPST, NTE, TOEFL and Adv. Practice are registered trademarks of ETS.
SAT is a registered trademark of CEEB.

Cliffs
NOTES.